RE-IMAGINING INTERNATIONAL RELATIONS

Buzan and Acharya challenge the discipline of International Relations to reimagine itself in the light of the thinking about, and practice of, international relations and world order from premodern India, China and the Islamic world. This pre-quel to their 2019 book, The Making of Global International Relations, takes the story back from the two-century tale of modern IR, to reveal the deep global history of the discipline. It shows the multiple origins and meanings of many concepts thought of as only modern and Western. It opens pathways for the rest of the world into this most Eurocentric of disciplines, encouraging them to bring their own histories, concepts and theories with them. The authors have written this book with the hope of inspiring others to extend these pathways by bring-ing in a wider array of cultures, and exploring how they thought about and acted in worlds composed of multiple, inde-pendent, collective actors.

Barry Buzan is Emeritus Professor of International Relations at the LSE (formerly Montague Burton Professor); honorary pro-fessor at Copenhagen, Jilin, and China Foreign Affairs Universities; a Senior Fellow at LSE Ideas; and a Fellow of the British Academy.

Amitav Acharya is the UNESCO Chair in Transnational Challenges and Governance and Distinguished Professor at the School of International Service, American University, Washington, DC. He is a Past President of the International Studies Association (ISA) and has won ISA Distinguished Scholar Awards (for contribution to study of International Organization and Non-Western International Relations).

Re-imagining International Relations

World Orders in the Thought and Practice of Indian, Chinese, and Islamic Civilizations

BARRY BUZAN
London School of Economics and Political Science

AMITAV ACHARYA
American University, Washington DC

CAMBRIDGE
UNIVERSITY PRESS

University Printing House, Cambridge CB2 8BS, United Kingdom

One Liberty Plaza, 20th Floor, New York, NY 10006, USA

477 Williamstown Road, Port Melbourne, VIC 3207, Australia

314–321, 3rd Floor, Plot 3, Splendor Forum, Jasola District Centre, New Delhi - 110025, India

103 Penang Road, #05–06/07, Visioncrest Commercial, Singapore 238467

Cambridge University Press is part of the University of Cambridge.

It furthers the University's mission by disseminating knowledge in the pursuit of education, learning, and research at the highest international levels of excellence.

www.cambridge.org
Information on this title: www.cambridge.org/9781316513859
DOI: 10.1017/9781009076197

First published 2022

A catalogue record for this publication is available from the British Library.

ISBN 978-1-316-51385-9 Hardback
ISBN 978-1-009-07491-9 Paperback

CONTENTS

FOREWORD

This book is an outgrowth and extension of our 2019 book, where the question of what International Relations (IR) would look like if it had been invented elsewhere was raised briefly in the Introduction (Acharya and Buzan, 2019: 3). Our 2019 book went on to look in some detail at modern, nineteenth and twentieth century, thinking about IR in Africa, Asia, the Middle East, and Latin America, unsurprisingly finding that most of it was about reactions to the racism, cultural contempt, violence, and imperialism of the Western powers plus Japan. In this book, we want to start looking behind that, to investigate thinking and practice from Indian, Chinese, and Islamic civilizations about IR and world order *before* their encounter with Europe and industrial modernity. What is the deeper background of thinking about world order and international relations that these civilizations are bringing, and will bring, to both re-imagining, and practising, international relations?

We would like to thank John Haslam for his interest and support, and especially the three reviewers for Cambridge University Press. They not only understood in depth what the book was trying to do but also provided us with a wealth of knowledgeable, and constructively critical, suggestions as to how to improve it. We are most grateful for their insights.

1 INTRODUCTION

It is not controversial to say that a small group of mainly Western powers, plus Russia and Japan, have dominated world politics since the early nineteenth century (Buzan and Lawson, 2015). Neither is it controversial to say that the modern discipline of International Relations (IR), which grew up during that period, has been largely shaped by that experience (Acharya and Buzan, 2019). Much of its thinking rests on the assumption that, in all the ways that matter, Western history more or less is world history. It is a story, and a way of thinking, told by the winners, and that is the basis for the potent charge of Eurocentrism made against it. We take that charge seriously for two reasons. First, there are other stories and ways of thinking about IR that have been overridden by Western dominance. If we are to build a more properly global discipline of IR, or what we call Global IR, we need to bring those stories in. Second, the period of Western dominance is now coming to an end, and the fabric of the winners' story of IR is wearing thin not only around the edges but in the middle. Those with other stories are re-emerging as centres of wealth, power, and cultural authority. As they do so, they bring their own stories, concepts, and ways of thinking into the contemporary practice of, and thinking about, IR. These marginalized stories and ways of understanding are thus being reinserted into the contemporary world order, with China, India, and the Islamic world being in the vanguard.

The aim of this book is to uncover these marginalized stories by conducting reconnaissance missions into the thinking and practice of international relations/world order in India, China, and the Islamic world. This aim can be understood in two ways. First, it uncovers what IR theory might look like had it been developed within civilizations other than the West. This is not just an eccentric, if entertaining, venture into alternative history. The main reason for attempting it is that, as we have argued at length in earlier works (Buzan, 2011; Acharya, 2014; Buzan and Lawson, 2015; Acharya and Buzan, 2019), this question has profound implications for both the contemporary practice of international relations and the academic discipline whose job it is to think about and theorize that practice. Second, it opens the door to rethinking the history, concepts, and theories of modern IR. Do these previously marginalized stories and ways of thinking share much common ground with modern IR, or do they challenge it in basic ways? Are concepts shared, and if so do they carry the same meanings, or is the existing repertoire destabilized by alternatives reflecting different histories?

In our understanding, the international system/society is now rapidly moving into a structure of *deep pluralism*. By this we mean that substantial parts of the former periphery/colonial world are successfully acquiring modernity on their own terms and catching up with the West not just in wealth and power but also in the wielding of cultural and political authority. In many places, that new wealth and power, and recovered cultural authority, are already significant enough to pose military, economic, legal, social, and political challenges to the West. In addition, they are widely linked to a still strongly felt postcolonial resentment: to get a measure of this one has only to look at the importance China still attaches not only to remembering its 'century of humiliation' but also to making it an active factor in its day-to-day foreign and domestic policy. By contrast, while public opinion in the West remains sensitive to racism in its domestic spheres and histories, it has largely forgotten about, or marginalized, the racism and coercion it exercised against other peoples during the imperial era, even though white nationalists within it are re-legitimizing racism in relation to contemporary migration. When Hedley Bull (1984) worried about the Third Worlds' 'revolt against the West' nearly forty years ago, that revolt could still be, and largely was, ignored because the newly decolonized states and peoples behind it were mostly poor, weak, and culturally emasculated. The West largely satisfied itself with some commitment to give foreign aid to the Third World in the hope that development along liberal lines would somehow be easy and automatic. Modernization theory assumed that modernization effectively meant Westernization (Spruyt, 2020: 344–6). Now, substantial parts of the former periphery are growing strong and knocking on the door of the core. They are finding, or in some cases such as China, South Korea, Taiwan, and Singapore have found, their own paths to modernity, and they are not clones of the West but distinctive syntheses between their traditional cultures and modernity. Their historical grievances against the West and Japan can no longer be sidelined.

The era of Western domination, when a handful of first-round modernizers, mostly white, European countries plus Japan, dominated the international system/society and shaped it for their own interests and preferences, is visibly coming to an end all around us. A new and novel international structure is emerging in which the homogenizing effects of shared modernity are accompanied by growing cultural and political differentiation. Capitalism won the Cold War, not liberal democracy, and all of the major powers are now capitalist in some sense. This outcome makes a big change from the world order before 1989. But that shared capitalism is differentiated into many political forms, ranging from democratic to authoritarian (Buzan and Lawson, 2014), and reflects different cultures across the spectrums from individualist to collectivist and from hierarchical to egalitarian. The resulting dialectics are embedded in the highly interconnected and interdependent world that the West created. The emerging world order of deep pluralism is not only powered by the spread and deepening of modernity but the very unfolding of modernity is now generating shared fate problems on a global scale from climate change and disease control, through mass extinctions and pollution, to economic management, cybersecurity, and terrorism.

This transition of the global international system/society to deep pluralism poses profound challenges to IR as a discipline. As we argued in our recent book (Acharya and Buzan, 2019), modern thinking about IR over the last two centuries has quite closely followed the practice of international relations.[1] To be blunt about it, and as is often pointed out by postcolonial scholars, this has resulted in IR being a highly Eurocentric discipline. It is not just a notable irony that the discipline designed to study humankind as a whole should be so parochial in its perspective, it is an existential problem in urgent need of correction.

The reasons for this situation are clear. The modern discipline of IR was formed during the last two centuries, exactly coinciding with the time when Western civilization became dominant and imposed itself on all the others. That imposition created a kind of overlay during which, for the first time in history, one civilization became not only fully global but also hegemonic. The modern discipline of IR was developed precisely when the West had the whip hand over everybody else, and this conjuncture inevitably made it Eurocentric. From the mid-nineteenth to the early twenty-first century, it could plausibly be argued that Western history and particularly the political economy of modernity led by the Anglosphere had in important respects become world history and global political economy.

Whether that was true or not, what mattered was that it was widely believed to be true in the West and accepted as substantially true by many modernizers elsewhere, who saw their job as trying to acquire modernity in order to restore their wealth,

---

[1] We make a quite sharp distinction between modern IR thinking, which got going during the nineteenth century, and pre-modern thinking about it, which largely reflected the concerns of agrarian, dynastic, and mostly imperial, polities. For the arguments supporting this view, see Buzan and Lawson (2015), Acharya and Buzan (2019), and Buzan and Lawson (forthcoming).

power, and status against the West. Speaking about nineteenth-century Japan, R. Taggart Murphy (2014: 63) brilliantly summarizes the extent of the challenge posed by the Western 'standard of civilization' to non-Western states and peoples:

The Meiji leaders faced three urgent and intertwined tasks. They had to build a military strong enough to act as a deterrent to Western imperialism. They had to assemble the capital and technology needed to turn their country into an industrial power sufficiently advanced to equip that military. And they had to create the institutions necessary not only to accomplish these other tasks but to convince the West that Japan had accumulated the prerequisites for membership in the club of countries that were to be taken seriously. That meant not only a credible military – preferably evidenced by victories in imperialist wars waged on weaker lands – but also such institutions as parliaments, courts, banks, monogamy, elections, and ideally, Christian churches, not to mention familiarity with Western ways and appearances in such matters as architecture, dress, sexual mores, and table manners. It was only by governing as leaders of a convincing imitation of a modern imperialist nation that these men could persuade the West to revise the Unequal Treaties and thereby wrest back control over their country's tariff regime and security apparatus from the Europeans.

Modern IR was founded, and evolved, during this entirely singular moment in world history, and it is thus neither surprising nor a matter for retrospective moral condemnation that as a consequence the discipline was cast in a Eurocentric form. Under the circumstances of the time, it is difficult to imagine how things could have evolved otherwise. We see little point in condemning the past for not living up to the insights and moral values of the present. Now, however, it is more than past time to move on from these Eurocentric foundations, and to recast the discipline of IR in fully global terms. Failure to do so invites both academic and moral questions of a very serious kind.

Although an oversimplification, it remains broadly true that contemporary mainstream IR theory is still not much more than an abstraction of Western history interwoven with Western political theory both classical and modern. Realism is an abstraction from eighteenth-century European balance-of-power behaviour combined with sixteenth and seventeenth century, and indeed ancient Greek, political theory. Liberalism is an abstraction from nineteenth and twentieth-century Western intergovernmental organizations and theories of political economy. Marxism is an abstraction from another branch of nineteenth and twentieth-century European theory of political economy and historical sociology. The English School is an abstraction from nineteenth century European diplomatic behaviour and a long European tradition of legal theory resting on the assumption that all law, including international law, presupposes the existence of a society. Constructivism is not so obviously abstracted from Western practice but is drawn from Western philosophy of knowledge. Because IR came into being when the West quite literally either ruled or dominated the world, it has been largely built on the assumption that Western history and Western political theory *are* world history and world political theory. Now that those peculiar conditions are coming to an end, IR needs urgently to address itself to a much more pluralist world in which modernized cultures additional to the West are increasingly powerfully in play, both materially and ideationally. Whether IR could have, or should have, made this move earlier is, in our view, beside the point. It needs to do so now.

In this emerging world, several longstanding civilizations, most notably China, are steadily achieving the fusion between their traditional cultures and the revolutions of modernity that the West and Japan underwent during the nineteenth and twentieth centuries (Koyama and Buzan, 2019; Buzan and Lawson, 2020). This is not a revival of the pre-modern world of different classical civilizations but something quite different and new. Just as traditional Western and Japanese cultures were transformed by modernity into something very different, so too is modernity transforming other classical cultures. While all will share a substrate of modernity, each will have blended modernity and its own culture in a distinctive way. The well-established idea of multiple modernities (Eisenstadt, 2000) is now reshaping both the distribution of power and the nature of global international society.

A useful theoretical framing for capturing this development is Justin Rosenberg's (2010, 2013, 2016; Buzan and Lawson, 2016) work on uneven and combined development (UCD), which stands as an alternative to Kenneth Waltz's (1979: 76) theory. Both Waltz and Rosenberg see 'socialization and competition' as consequences of 'combination' (i.e., units interacting within the same system). But they disagree about their effects: Waltz famously favouring homogenization into 'like units' and Rosenberg arguing oppositely that the particular timing and circumstances of socialization and competition necessarily produce variable outcomes. The extreme conditions created by macro-historical transformations such as the one that took place during the long nineteenth century expose the logic of the latter with great clarity. Major transformations of this kind have a distinct point or points of origin in which a particular configuration emerges and is sustained. This configuration is produced and reproduced through inter-societal interactions across time and space, generating diverse outcomes. These interactions can be coercive, emulative, and/or reactive, and each social order that encounters the new configuration has its own way of adapting to it. Some social orders do not take on the new configuration at all, either because of internal resistance to the changes it requires or because of attempts by leading-edge polities to maintain inequalities between them by denying access to elements of the transformation. Others succeed in developing indigenous versions of the new configuration. 'Late' developers are not carbon copies of the original adopters but develop their own distinctive characteristics.

In this sense, the interactions between different social orders produce not convergence but (often unstable) amalgams of new and old. For example, during the nineteenth century, the

German and the American industrializations were not replicas of British development but took distinct forms, even as they borrowed from the British experience. Likewise, Soviet and, more recently, Chinese development also maintained their own characteristics, combining new technologies and productive forces alongside inherited social formations. Through the analytic lens of UCD, it becomes clear that development is multilinear rather than linear, proceeds in fits and starts rather than through smooth gradations, and contains many variations in terms of outcomes. One indicator of the ways in which polities adapted in diverse ways to the nineteenth-century global transformation is the variety of ideologies that have emerged to define different assemblages of economy, politics, and culture in the modern world: liberalism, social democracy, conservatism, socialism, communism, fascism, patrimonialism, and more.

UCD underlines how and why the deep pluralist world order now emerging from the ongoing spread and deepening of modernity will be as much – or more – culturally, economically, and politically differentiated as homogenized. This new configuration will reshape not just the practice of international relations but also how IR is thought about and theorized. We need to get some sense of what kinds of thinking about IR these newly transformed civilizations will bring with them. How will their ideas and concepts fit with, and/or compete with, the highly West-centric theoretical construction that the discipline of IR currently reflects?

In order to get this process underway, we take a first look at the thinking and practice about 'international relations', or more broadly 'world order', that went on in three major centres of classical civilization: China, India, and the Islamic world. For this purpose, *world order* is a broader and more useful concept. It does away with the word 'international', which is closely linked to the Westphalian type of interstate order, and helps us analyse the wider range of polities and the relationships among them that characterized the five millennia of world history that preceded modernity. Studying how classical civilizations understood world orders can broaden the study of IR in several ways. First, it helps us to understand, and if necessary challenge, the dominance of certain key ideas that claim to be universal and have largely been taken for granted in IR as such. This could be one way of addressing the problem of Eurocentrism in the discipline: for example, the dominance of Westphalian sovereignty, anarchy, and balance of power, which marginalizes other forms of statehood and international order building through history, such as empires or universal monarchy or universal peace.

Second, and conversely, the study of civilizations helps us to illustrate the multiple sources of key ideas such as human rights, international law, moral and functional norms, international institutions, and power politics. These concepts are often assumed to be derived from European history but may well have other origins. Understanding the global roots of key ideas in IR could make them appreciated as genuinely universal, and hence give them even greater importance and legitimacy. Third, the study of classical civilizations helps discover neglected or forgotten ideas, processes, and practices that have been ignored or understudied but are fundamental to understanding how the world works, past, present, and future. Examples of these are the Chinese *Tianxia*, Islam's synthesizing or bridging role between the East and the West, the Indian Maurya King Ashoka's idea of moral conquest, etc. While history may not repeat itself, it offers us a range of symbols and possibilities when we examine ideas and institutions of the past such as the hierarchical system/ society, empires, sovereign systems, and the tributary system. These ideas and practices might facilitate a better understanding of the behaviour of rising powers such as China, India, Iran, and Turkey. Their current leaders are invoking the past to explain and legitimize their current foreign policy and strategic behaviour, which in turn is a key element of contemporary world politics. At the same time, uncovering these ideas and practices enriches the repertoire of theory and method in IR and comparative politics. IR is not just about relationships of power and wealth. It is also about the flow of ideas and innovations. Studying IR from a historical-civilizational perspective opens the door to a greater under-standing of relationships based on the creation and diffusion of ideas and innovations.

The idea of world order gives a central place to the diffusion of cultures, ideas, and innovations that no serious student of IR should ignore. A world order can be hierarchic, such as an empire; anarchic, like the warring states of China, the pre-Mauryan republics of India, and the Greek city-states; or some-where in between, like the Chinese tribute system, where a leading state maintains a degree of control over other states' domestic and foreign relations but does not take away their sovereignty. Henry Kissinger (2014: 9) defines world order as a 'concept held by a region or civilization about the nature of just arrangements and the distribution of power thought to be applicable to the entire world'. Going by this definition, a world order is not the same as global order: it can be sub-global in scale. John King Fairbank (1968) coined the term 'Chinese World Order' on the grounds that the term 'international sys-tem' could not apply to China before the twentieth century when the country had not absorbed the notion of Westphalian sovereignty. Most world orders were created by civilizations that, while originating from a single country or region, achieved a transnational or transcontinental reach, whether through material (including conquest and trade) or ideational (often religious) means. A world order can be devel-oped by any civilization that imagines its ideas and institutions to be universal and timeless. Moreover, a world order is not just about the 'power' and 'just arrangements' that a civilization possesses. It is also, and even more, about its identity and interactions, meaning how civilizations see themselves as dis-tinctive entities and how they interact with both others seen as 'civilized' and others seen as 'barbarians'. Civilizations can be understood either as relatively closed, bounded, homogenous, exclusionary entities almost with actor quality or as relatively open, plural, fluid, inclusionary entities, with the former pointing towards othering, conflict, and war and the latter towards peaceful interaction and multiple identities (Katzenstein, 2010; Rudolph, 2010: 137, 148). In what follows, we apply both understandings as appropriate.

Our method is comparative history and political theory intertwined with some geopolitics. We choose India, China, and the Islamic world partly because they are a good fit with our knowledge base but mainly for two other reasons. First, these three civilizations are differently placed geopolitically within the Eurasian system, and therefore had different kinds of encounters and experiences with the other peoples, polities, and civilizations around them. For all of them, the experience of 'the international' was a mix of internal dynamics and external encounters. Second, all three are still a major presence in the current international system/society. Their traditions of thought about international relations as filtered through their encounters with modernity are therefore likely to affect both how they behave and what kind of impact their increasing involvement will make on the study and theorizing of IR. Indeed, increasingly there is IR literature from these countries, particularly China, that draws on their own history and political theory to think about IR. We can use this literature to get insight into not only how non-Western histories and political theories might be brought into contemporary IR but also how they actually already are being brought in. We hope that we provide a template that could be used by others to bring additional civilizations into the argument should people find it interesting and useful to do that.

We are acutely aware that this is in some respects an insanely ambitious exercise. We are under no illusions that we can either capture fully the experiences and outlooks of historical cultures and polities or track precisely how those factors have filtered through the experience of encounter and modernity to the present day. That said, we take hope from the substantial role that pre-modern Western thinkers from Thucydides and Plato to Hobbes and Machiavelli play in contemporary Western IR theorizing, which if nothing else shows that the past remains active in the present in terms of both practice and theory. The same could be said for the role of Confucius and other sages in Chinese, and Kautilya in Indian, thinking about world order. In what follows, we aim partly to locate and sketch other similar potential links in India, China, and the Islamic world but mainly to set up an agenda for further research by those with greater specific expertise than we possess. Our analysis cannot pretend to be definitive, but we hope it will inspire others to try to move it in that direction. We will next address some problems intrinsic to such an exercise, then look at our three cases, and finally draw some preliminary conclusions.

2 PROBLEMS WITH THE EXERCISE

Although there is quite a bit of empirical evidence to draw on, this kind of exercise is not straightforward, especially if the aim is the counterfactual one of understanding what non-Western 'IR' would look like if it had evolved from one of these three other civilizations. Before proceeding with our cases studies, there are five difficulties that need to be addressed:

1. How to handle the close link between the discipline of IR that we now have and the period of Western world dominance.
2. Does culture matter in international relations or is it all materialism?
3. How 'Western' is modern IR?
4. Can ancient and modern concepts and practices be equated?
5. Empires versus states, and how to differentiate inside and outside.

How to Handle the Close Link between the Discipline of IR That We Now Have and the Period of Western World Dominance

While it is possible to reconstruct the general background of how other classical civilizations thought about and practised 'international relations' before modernity, it is impossible, or at best extremely speculative, to think through the trajectories that could have either brought them to global domination in the way that happened for the West or allowed them to stand aside from that. Since modern IR theory emerged precisely during the period of both the first round of revolutions of modernity and Western world dominance, we cannot reproduce that experience for civilizations other than the West and Japan. Not only that but, as we show in our book (Acharya and Buzan, 2019), modern IR thinking from the nineteenth century onwards in Asia, the Middle East, Latin America, and Africa was, not surprisingly, almost entirely about how to resist and overcome the economic, colonial, and racist impositions of the West and Japan on the rest of the world. It was therefore more of a reaction to the huge disruption and cultural humiliation created by the combined encounter with Western and Japanese power and the revolutions of modernity than it was an expression of thinking about IR rooted in a different culture and history. That modern, reactive, trajectory, of course, remains in play today and is important in itself for understanding the evolution of modern IR thinking in terms of *dependencia*, postcolonial, and regionalist theory. And that reaction was itself somewhat shaped by how different cultures reacted to the dual encounter with the West and modernity.

But the reactive encounter mainly distracts from the purpose of teasing out what IR theory might look like if it had been developed by a civilization other than the West and one that had not been traumatized by an encounter with the West from a position of weakness. The colonial experience of the non-West, and their reactions against the humiliations of imperialism and racism, certainly shapes, and will continue to shape, how they think about international relations going forward. But it also, almost inevitably, reinforces the Eurocentric story around which IR is currently built. We want, as far as possible, to dig deeper by unearthing the kind of thinking about IR/world order that was going on in China, India, and the Islamic world before their encounter with the West and modernity. This is the foundation from which they might have projected an IR development rooted in histories and political theories other than the West's and not distorted by their encounter with it. It is also a significant part of the foundation from which people within these newly empowered civilizations will play into the practice of, and thinking about, contemporary IR. We want to aim for a separate sense of how both the specific postcolonial resentment and the wider historical and philosophical background, might play into contemporary and future IR thinking and theorizing. Our main focus is therefore on the thinking and practices that lie behind the reactions against Western and Japanese colonialism and racism.

Does Culture Matter in International Relations?

Here the difficulty is that our whole exercise rests on the assumption that culture and history matter to how international relations is, or might be, theorized. Those of a materialist disposition, such as neorealists, neoliberals, and Marxists, might well question this assumption. In their perspective, the realm of international relations might be understood as having particular structural qualities that privilege material factors over social ones. They treat international relations as a *system*, with all the mechanical implications that term carries. Even for those not ideologically wedded to materialism, the systemic approach has specific appeal for the realm of the international. While the realm inside states and other polities might be thought of as social, ordered, and progressive, the realm outside them is more mechanical and repetitive. As Martin Wight (1966: 26) memorably put it, the domestic realm is one where progress is possible, while 'International politics is the realm of recurrence and repetition'. If it is the case that the international realm is marked by extremely weak social and political structures, and consequently generates a high probability of conflict among whatever kinds of units compose it, then it might well display a relatively unchanging mechanical character.

If this is in fact the case, then we might not learn much from looking at the thinking about, and practice of, international relations within different cultures. Regardless of their domestic characters and differences, all would face a risky, uncertain, and generally hostile outside environment to which they would have to either react appropriately or succumb. This line of thought would suggest that it does not matter much that the discipline of IR arose within one particular civilization at one particular time. Except in rare cases of utopian isolation, where a civilization had no neighbours of consequence, similar circumstances would have been faced by all civilizations at all times. All would live in hostile and threatening systems, which would force prioritization of self-preservation through strength, and we would therefore expect thinking about, and practice of, international relations to take a broadly similar, and mainly realist/power politics, form across both temporal and cultural differentiations. Western IR would not be particularly distinctive just because it was Western and might well have uncovered, or rediscovered, most if not all of whatever truths about IR are there to be found.

Like Hendrick Spruyt (2020), we do not think it is the case that IR can be treated mainly as a material phenomenon, as if it were a branch of physics. But our approach allows this perspective to be treated as a hypothesis and should enable us to make some judgement on the question one way or another. If we find that thinking about and practising international relations/world order in civilizations other than the West nonetheless take a broadly similar form, then Wight's idea of a 'realm of recurrence and repetition' will be supported. If, however, culture does matter in international relations, then we would expect to find substantial differentiation in how world order/international relations has been thought about and practised across time and space. For this reason, we use the hybrid term *international system/ society* to allow room for both understandings.

How 'Western' Is Modern IR?

What we think of as Western IR[1] may in fact have picked up a lot of ideas from other cultures and therefore in that sense

---

[1] From the very outset, we want to remind readers, as we have done in all our work on 'non-Western IR' or 'Global IR', that the terms 'West' and 'non-West' are problematic and controversial labels. As we (Acharya and Buzan, 2007:

may not be strictly European. Europe's ascent to world power defines much of modern history and is in that sense the latest in a line of civilizations that have thought about the problems posed by international relations. It would therefore be natural that the latest in line would have incorporated at least some, and possibly quite a lot, of the earlier thinking from other civilizations. That possibility is enhanced by the fact that the European ascendency was done on a global scale and by a culture energized by scientific modernity and eager to learn as much as it could about the cultures it conquered and subordinated. Europeans were quite used to learning from the past and had put the extensive intellectual heritage from ancient Greece and Rome at the centre of their culture. As Daniel Deudney (2007: 91) puts it, 'Action and words from classical Greece and republican Rome stand enshrined as foundational in the modern conception of the West as a distinct civilization, and ancient writers and events have exercised a startlingly powerful presence in all aspects of Western thought, particularly about politics'. There is a nice irony here, because Greece, and through it Rome, drew heavily on the civilizations of Mesopotamia and Egypt that both preceded and ran in parallel with them. Indeed, classical Greece and Rome were more part of a Mediterranean civilization with strong links to Africa, Mesopotamia, and South and Central Asia, and weaker ones to China, than a strictly European one. Europe's chosen classical roots thus already run deeply into other civilizations.

431–2) argued in 2007, the 'West/non-West distinction', might seem 'old-fashioned, confrontational, and misleading given the diversity that undoubtedly exists within both camps' and that it was 'not possible to give any concrete or precise definition to what constitutes non-Western, not the least because it would involve making judgements about what is "West"'. Yet differences between North and South continued to exist, covering material, ideational and institutional resources that influence the study of IR. IR is developing both global/international and regional/local tracks. But overall, these distinctions are better viewed as 'terms of convenience' (Acharya, 2011: 621); we very much realize and accept that the boundaries between the two are often arbitrary and fluid. Other scholars such as Tickner and Wæver (2009: 3, 332) and Shilliam (2009), have also used Western and non-Western with reservation and nuance.

Despite their openness to, and respect for, the wisdom of ancient Greece and Rome, nineteenth-century Europeans often held pre-modern 'native' peoples in contempt on racial, religious, and cultural grounds. They thought of themselves as 'civilized' and others as being 'barbarian' or 'savage'. Yet, it was also the case that during their eighteenth and nineteenth-century encounters with Asian civilizations, the British learned a lot about textiles and steel from India and porcelain-making from China and that eighteenth-century European reformers were impressed by the meritocratic quality of China's mandarinate bureaucracy (Braudel, 1994 [1987]: 188–90, 194; Buzan and Lawson, 2015: 26, 31). To the extent that Europeans incorporated IR thinking from either or both the ancient Mediterranean world and the other civilizations they encountered during the European expansion, that would make the modern discipline of IR less specifically Western in character than is usually supposed. In that case, the apparent Eurocentrism of IR's 1919 founding story centred on the Anglosphere, its eccentric and parochial key 'modern' date of 1648, its ideas about power politics and liberal economic orders, and its promotion of its own history as world history might be Eurocentric only in a fairly superficial sense, masking cosmopolitan origins that are anything but Eurocentric. This factor too, could generate a degree of similarity between 'Western' IR thinking and that done in other cultures at other times. We might not be able to track the genealogy of such derivations directly, but we can certainly look for parallels that might make that tracking task a worthwhile research project for those more suitably qualified for it than we are.

Can Ancient and Modern Concepts and Practices Be Equated?

In pursuing this exercise, we need to remain sensitive to the issue of 'tempocentrism': the backward projection of modern concepts, such as sovereignty, power, norms, human rights, democracy, balance of power, rationality, and suchlike to the past. The temptation to do this is strong in IR because it opens the way to establishing the uniformity, continuity, and universality of modern concepts and theories derived from recent European history. We are conscious that while IR theory often purports to speak in a universal linguistic code, many of the core concepts of IR theory vocabulary– such as power, sovereignty, balancing, peace, empire, norms – derive directly or indirectly (e.g., via old French) from Greek and Latin. Hellenocentrism or Græco-Roman centrism are in some ways precursors of Eurocentrism, but in other ways they connect European thinking to the wider Eurasian cultural circuits with which Greece and Rome were linked. How do we recognize the cultural and historical sources and contexts of existing concepts so that they do not become part of an artificial universal code that ignores or obscures other origins? This is a challenging task for Global IR today.

To understand hegemony, you start with Greek *hegemonia*, and think of the Hellenistic world, which was a world where legitimizing ideas spread with the backing of competition and force. To understand empire, you think of *imperium* and *imperator*, and Rome as the archetypal empire, with all its violent direct political control. Yet if you think of the spread of ideas in Asia, the situation is different: Indian ideas mostly spread to Southeast Asia and East Asia without the backing of force and the Chinese imperium flourished for long periods more by symbolic authority than brute physical force.

The Greek notion of *hegemonia* has multiple meanings, but as David Wilkinson (2008: 119) notes, it largely implies 'military-political hierarchy, not one of wealth or cultural prestige'. Hellenization, the spread of classical Greek culture, started with Greek migration, which did sometimes lead to the displacement of the original inhabitants of where the Greeks went, such as Sicily. Later Hellenization, with Alexander the Great, came on the back of direct military conquest. By contrast, the spread of Indian and Chinese ideas, especially the former, was more due to their cultural prestige, and 'Indianization' was largely a pacific process that did not produce the displacement of local societies but instead led to their cultural and political enhancement (Acharya, 2012: 60–70).

To compound matters, other languages may not have the equivalent meaning to these core concepts. The Chinese are often puzzled by the steady stream of words that the West uses to deal with them that have no equivalent in their own language – such as 'engagement', 'confidence-building', 'human security'. They even do not have an exact equivalent of 'sovereignty' (*zhu quan* or master/patron rights). For them, 'engagement', a favourite policy term of the United States, is *jie chu*, meaning 'touch and connect'. The term 'security' is translated as *an quan* in Chinese, but this exact Chinese term can also be used for 'safety', which has a less military connotation.[2] As a leading Chinese scholar, Qin Yaqing, points out, the Chinese traditionally had no sense of 'international-ness' as understood in the West,[3] so how do they relate to the discipline of International Relations? In response, the Chinese have come up with their own terms such as *Tianxia* (all under heaven) and *datong* (universal great harmony), among others, to describe their worldview. There are also more politically charged concepts such as 'peaceful rise', 'peaceful development', 'convergence of interests', 'harmonious relations', and 'community of common destiny'. While their deployment may be self-serving (Zhao, S., 2017), it is not entirely different to the purposes for which the West's 'democratic peace' or 'liberal hegemony' are employed. As we show in the chapters that follow, many states and societies provide examples of ideas that resonate with both idealistic and power politics ways of thinking, making their association with existing English language concepts possible and explorable, though not easy.

---

[2] We are grateful to Shanshan Mei and Di Wu, research scholars at American University, for these translations and clarifications.

[3] This is in the specific context of the tributary system: 'Such a system had no room for "international-ness". Traditionally, therefore, Chinese had no consciousness of "international-ness" and concepts related with it such as sovereignty and territorial integrity. It was natural that there was no need to develop a theory of IR' (Qin, 2007: 323–34).

One has to be careful and alert to the possibility that contemporary concepts may not have existed in the past, or may have existed in different forms with different meaning and significance. They may not exist across cultures. At the same time, we do not rule out the possibility either that materialists have a point about the 'recurrence and repetition' of international relations indicating the operation of deep structures or that 'Western' IR thinking has borrowed ideas across time and space. If these factors operate in any significant sense, there may well be parallel or analogous concepts across cultures. But we do not take this as a given, and we pay close attention to the cultural context of such concepts where we find them.

Hence, we are conscious that using labels such as anarchy, hierarchy, idealism, realism, rationality, norms, interdependence, and globalization, etc. may make us seem West-centric because they are used widely in Western academic and policy discourses. But our goal is precisely the opposite. We do not think one needs to dump these concepts entirely and deploy a wholly new vocabulary to investigate or 'bring in' non-Western contributions to IR, lest one commits the same sin of Eurocentrism. That argument is simplistic and flawed. It wrongly assumes that these concepts, or the structures, institutions, and practices they represent, are uniquely Western contributions, an impression reinforced by the fact that they are often presented that way, partly due to the dominance of the English language (which has borrowed some of these concepts from Greek and Roman as well as other civilizations). In fact, one aim of this book is to challenge the claim of the West to have invented them or IR in general. Relatedly, the key concepts which are investigated here are generic ideas about world politics and order and can be used with their dictionary meanings, rather than being peculiarly part of the Western politics and IR lexicon. They represent very broad understandings of politics and order in domestic and international relations, whether ancient or modern. Hence using them as points of reference and comparison is both convenient and useful.

For example, a leading Chinese IR scholar, Yan Xuetong (2011: 14) cautions against blandly applying modern categories of 'realist' or 'idealist' to differentiate between Chinese philosophers but still finds enough nuanced parallels between the classical thinkers and modern political science and IR concepts to associate Confucianism with idealism, Laozi with anarchism, Mozi with pacifism, Hanfeizi with realism, and Xunzi (and himself) with 'moral realism'. As he puts it, 'The language and vocabulary of the pre-Qin thinkers were very different from those used today, yet their way of thinking about problems and their logic were very similar' (Yan, 2011: 26).

This is not to deny that some of these concepts have different meanings in different historical and cultural contexts. Nor is it to deny that there are concepts and ideas in non-Western societies that are entirely new to the existing vocabulary of IR. The discipline needs to think hard about what challenges these raise to its orthodoxies and how to incorporate or adapt to them in order to make IR theory genuinely universal. But if the development of IR is to be a truly global conversation, Western and non-Western scholars need to speak to rather than speak past each other. To do so, they need to develop and use a shared vocabulary. This means and requires that Western scholars should develop an understanding of non-Western concepts just as they expect non-Western scholars to be well-versed in Western ideas. It is only through this mutual learning and engagement that one can advance the possibility of a truly Global IR. So, what we seek to present in this book is an attempt to steer the conversation about the future of IR in that direction.

In pursuing a Global IR approach, one obvious temptation would be to try to fit local experiences into existing theoretical categories, Realism, Liberalism, Constructivism, Marxism, English School, etc., or into concepts such as sovereignty, balance of power, interdependence, international society, etc. But this is not satisfactory, as one might lose the original sense and context of these concepts. Moreover, many vernacular concepts may fall beyond or actually straddle the realist–liberal–constructivist divide, which itself is being increasingly challenged within recent theoretical IR literature, especially by those who call for 'analytic eclecticism' (Sil and Katzenstein, 2010). Some vernacular concepts may not have any equivalent in the English language.

Another approach, not mutually exclusive with the previous one, would be similar to what some IR scholars call 'vernacularization' or 'translation', that is, applying existing theoretical concepts in different historical and contemporary local settings with particular emphasis on ascertaining how their meanings vary and change in those settings. At the extreme end, such an effort could involve 'constitutive localization' (Acharya, 2004, 2012), whereby reinterpretations of universal concepts are made on the basis of local 'cognitive priors', with the end result accentuating local meanings and practices over outside ones.

A third approach, again not mutually exclusive with the above two, would be to present concepts and approaches from different parts of the world on their own terms. At the same time, some way of relating these vernacular concepts to existing theories may be helpful in making them more 'recognizable' to the entire IR community, while preserving the vernacular concepts' *autonomous* meanings and highlighting their *associated* meanings (meanings of association with existing IR concepts). While theories such as Realism, Liberalism, Constructivism, English School, etc. are Western in origin and context, concepts underlying these theories, such as power, interest, justice, peace, resistance, international and world society, etc., are more universal notions which can be found in most cultures and languages in some form. In other words, different cultures and regions may offer similar but not the same concepts. The answer must involve exploring to some degree both the autonomous and associated meanings of key IR concepts.

Empires versus States, and How to Differentiate Inside and Outside

Related to the difficulty over mismatched meanings and concepts just discussed is the problem that the dominant unit against which modern IR has been defined is the modern, rational state (Buzan and Lawson, 2015: 127–70). The modern state makes a fetish of sovereignty, territoriality, and nationalism and therefore of hard, and relatively fixed, borders. As a consequence, modern IR is defined in terms of a clear distinction between inside and outside (Wight, 1966; Walker, 1993). By contrast, the dominant unit in our three pre-modern case studies is what Buzan and Lawson (forthcoming: ch. 4–6) call conglomerate agrarian/pastoralist empires (CAPEs). As Robert Gilpin (1981: 110–15) sketches out, these are a quite different type of entity from the modern state. They have loose, conglomerate structures and fluctuating and vague boundaries that simply do not permit the strict differentiation between inside and outside that characterizes IR in Westphalian systems. Such empires typically go through cycles of expansion and disintegration, though the pace of these cycles varies a lot. Some CAPEs lasted a long time (Han, Roman, Byzantine, Abbasid, Ottoman, Qing), while others were quite ephemeral (Alexander's, Qin, Seljuk). Writers of the time, such as Kautilya, Ibn Khaldun, and Nizam al Mulk (on whom more in Chapter 6) were all far more focused on the expansion and fall processes internal to empires than on their outside relations with others of their kind.

Such empires certainly did have inside/outside 'international relations', most obviously, but not only, with other, rival empires. Empires also had to relate to the more or less autonomous merchants whose guilds and diasporas managed long-distance trade. Sometimes they had to deal with migrating and/or invading nomadic tribes on a scale that could be militarily and politically threatening.

There are many examples of inter-imperial relations, particularly in the crowded civilizational world of the Mediterranean and Middle East: Athens and Sparta, Rome and Carthage, Rome and Parthia, Byzantium and Sassanid, Ottoman and Habsburg, Ottoman and Safavid, Ottoman and Russia, etc. Yet, because of their loose and layered political structure and their fluid and often ambiguous outer boundaries, it is difficult to differentiate their 'domestic' politics from 'international' relations. As observed so closely by Khaldun, within such empires, relations between core and periphery could and did loosen or tighten frequently. Such empires were often put together in a pyramidal form, with local rulers being left in place to govern under the watchful eye (and imperial garrisons) of the centre. That kind of political structure meant that CAPEs could be put together quickly and at low cost. But it also meant that when the centre weakened, they could equally quickly fall apart as local polities pulled away. Empires were mainly extractive, but they did also provide collective goods such as law, currency, trade, and security. Mostly they did not attempt to homogenize cultures or identities, though they sometimes had this effect through the provision of a lingua franca, a script, a legal code, and/or a religion.

Thus, given territories might sometimes be inside an empire, sometimes outside it, or in only the most tenuous relationship with it – for example, the Barbary states and Egypt with the Ottoman Empire during the nineteenth century, or Afghanistan between the Safavid and the Mughal empires. An empire could be, and often was, a kind of international system in its own right. One could easily see 'universal' empires, such as Rome and Han China, which incorporated most or all of their local 'known world' as being international system/societies that fluctuated between conditions of anarchy and hierarchy. Many of the more successful agrarian empires liked to think of themselves as, in principle, universal in the sense that their rulers could potentially incorporate the whole world. That is why the Chinese concept of *Tianxia* mentioned above stands so strongly in contrast to Westphalian ideas of segmented territoriality.

This kind of unit was dominant throughout the world up to the nineteenth century, and even within the modern era remained a major force up until 1945. It provides a very different basis from the modern state for thinking about, conceptualizing and practising international relations and world order. Perhaps the main similarity between the two types of dominant unit is that both were typically embedded in, and dependent on, trading systems much more extensive than themselves. Modern states spawned a global system of trade and finance that ensnared all. Classical empires sometimes tried to capture their trading system and internalize it, but seldom if ever succeeded. The Chinese never captured the whole of the Silk Roads, and Roman senators complained about the drainage of specie to Asia to pay for imports of luxury goods such as silk (Buzan and Little, 2000: 222).

The Plan of the Book

It is beyond the scope of this rather exploratory and preliminary study to try to provide genealogies linking pre-modern thinking and practice with the vocabulary of contemporary IR theory. If this book generates debate, then others better qualified than we are might want to develop that angle. Our aim is to look for similarities and differences in the way world order and international relations have been thought about and practised across time and space. In doing that, we want to avoid any unnecessary privileging of the current vocabulary and theory of contemporary IR, while at the same time finding sufficient common ground to make comparisons and explore differences. To that end, we deploy a relatively neutral scheme of six terms and headings under which we can classify both the thinking and practice that we find. The first five of these are, we think, generic to almost any system of relationships that would fit the framings of 'international relations' and 'world orders': *hierarchy, power politics, peaceful coexistence, international political economy*, and *territoriality/transnationalism*. The sixth, *modes of thinking*, also applies across both thinking and practice but highlights the normative and philosophical framings used to think about this subject.

- By *hierarchy*, we mean the disposition to think that, and act as if, social relations are necessarily and preferably structured by rank order rather than a principle of equality. The criteria for this rank-ordering are varied and include class, race, wealth, power, and ideology. Hierarchy can work at all levels of society from domestic (slavery, patriarchy, aristocracy, apartheid, etc.) to international (standard of civilization, great power rights and responsibilities, imperialism/colonialism).

- By *power politics*, we mean the disposition to think that, and act as if, social relations, including particularly 'international' ones, are mainly driven by the desire of actors to accumulate wealth, power, security, and status for themselves. Until the rise of nationalism during the nineteenth century, the main expressions of this were empire and dynasticism, which made it legitimate for rulers to acquire slaves, subjects, loot, and territory by force.

- By *peaceful coexistence* we mean the thinking and practice around a wide range of strategies, structures, and conditions, from recognition and diplomacy to cooperation on joint projects, with which a group of polities can move their relations away from zero-sum power politics.[4] Empire and group identities such as religion can be means for peaceful coexistence, though they can also support power politics and/or hierarchy.

- By *international political economy* we mean the disposition to think of, and act as if, trade and commerce as activities are desirable in themselves and to some extent separable from politics and war.

- By *territoriality/transnationalism* we mean the disposition to think or act in such a way as either to link politics and

---

[4] Our notion of *peaceful coexistence* should not be confused with the contemporary notion of the 'Five Principles of Peaceful Coexistence' (*Panchasheel* in Hindi), which were agreed between China and India in 1953–4. Those were 'mutual respect for sovereignty and territorial integrity, mutual non-aggression, non-interference in each other's internal affairs, equality and mutual benefit, and peaceful coexistence' (Backgrounder, 2015). These principles, which are still emphasized in Chinese foreign policy, are based on modern Westphalian principles of sovereignty, equality and non-interference, which were largely absent in classical Asia. Our context is one of empires, suzerainty, and hierarchy, and our usage of *peaceful coexistence* has broader, especially normative and cultural elements, although both concepts seek to limit zero-sum power politics.

culture to territory, or not. This dyad also applies to the economic sector. Transnational thought and action opens space for non-state actors and human beings individually or in groups to be players in international relations/world order.

- By *modes of thinking* we mean different ways of understanding and analysing human behaviour, and specifically concepts and theories relating directly to IR and relevant ideas about epistemology.

In the case studies that follow, we hope to cast light on all of these issues and to return to them in more detail in the conclusions. Our expectation is that it would be amazing if we did not find some significant similarities across time and space in thinking about, and practising, international relations. Realists are not wrong to argue that the logics of power and survival have a certain structural universality. But we would be equally amazed, if we found no significant differences. Culture and circumstance have varied very widely across history, and it would be singular triumph for materialist, structural logic if this did not generate distinctive lines of thinking about, and practising, world order and international relations.

In what follows, we order our case studies chronologically beginning with India, then China, and finally the Islamic world. India has the historically older civilization (the Indus Valley) and, like China, has been a continuous civilization. Both experienced periodic rule by foreign powers, and both managed successfully to absorb foreign influences. As India's Prime Minister Jawaharlal Nehru put it, despite the fact that 'India was divided and conquered many times in history ... always the idea of the political unity of India persisted' (Nehru, 1938). The view that Indian civilization is discontinuous, unlike China's, ignores that fact that the ideas and rituals of Vedic India (mid-second millennium BC, contemporary of China's Shang and Zhou) are still extant today in the daily lives of Hindu Indians. The Islamic world was a relative latecomer. Whereas China, India, and to a lesser extent Europe had deep and continuous connections with indigenous historical roots, Islamic civilization built on the foundations of an array of civilizations that had preceded it in the same territories: Egyptian, Mesopotamian, Persian, Greek, Roman, Byzantine, Hindu. It was what Fernand Braudel (1994 [1987]: 41–3) calls a 'successor civilization'.

In all three cases, we look at both the *thinking* about, and the *practice* of, international relations. We do this both to find sources for a hypothetical IR coming out of that experience and to enrich understanding of what these concepts might contain beyond the specific Western readings that now dominate them in IR. This dual sourcing is also foundational to Western IR, which is as much, or possibly more, built on the observation of historical practice as on the abstractions of political theorists. We try to identify thinking through key written sources and to observe how thinking and practice do or don't line up. We try to relate all this to the particular geopolitical circumstances that shaped each case. The general structure of the three case-study chapters that follow is to start by introducing the geopolitical setting, then look at what the key written sources have to say, and finally consider practice, and how it does or doesn't line up with the thinking. We concentrate the main discussion of modes of thinking under the heading of 'thinking' and bring in the other five concepts as appropriate throughout. The cases are all aimed towards a set of comparative conclusions in Chapter 6.

3 INDIA

Introduction

One difficulty in dividing up our three cases as we have done is, of course, that classical 'India', especially after the rise of the Mughal empire early in the sixteenth century, but also substantially before that, is also part of the Islamic world. This was especially the case with northern India, although the Delhi sultanate and the Mughals did sometimes extend their reach deep into South India. In this chapter, therefore, we will focus on pre-Mughal – mainly Vedic, Buddhist, and Hindu – India, discussing the Mughal empire in the following chapter as part of the Islamic world. There is a strong case for seeing the Mughal empire, and the Delhi sultanate before it, with their Mongol-Turkic elites, their strong linkages to Persian culture and administration, and their transnational connection to the *umma*, as being part of the Islamic world (Dale, 2010). There is a good deal of politicized debate and speculation about the 'indigeneity' of the Indian civilization.[1] One question is whether, or to what extent, the Indus Valley people were native to the region or the product of earlier waves of migration from Western and Central Asia. Also contentious is the relationship between the Indus Valley civilization and the subsequent civilization founded in the Ganges Valley around the middle to late second millennium BC by the inflow of Central Asian nomads (the so-called Aryans).[2] Did the Indus Valley society maintain any continuity with the subsequent West Asian migrants?

---

[1] For an overview, see Menon and Mishra (2013).
[2] The popular narrative is that nomadic 'Aryans' drove out the indigenous population of north India (called the 'Dravidians') to the south. A counter-argument is that there was no displacement but intermixing.

There is little question that India's civilization and political order was crucially shaped throughout its history by its location in the middle of the Eurasian system, which made it more exposed than other parts of southern or eastern Asia to direct contact with other civilizations, especially those to its west. At the same time, like both China and the Islamic world, South Asia was from an early point also under pressure from militarily superior pastoralist steppe nomads (Scott, 2017: 183–9; Neumann and Wigen, 2018). 'Aryan' nomads began moving into India from around 1500 BC. This was a conflictual process with the local inhabitants, although recent research and excavations suggest that the 'Aryans' did not totally displace the pre-existing Indus Valley civilization but might have absorbed elements of its culture and people. By 600 BC, this process had produced a hybrid culture and the caste system, one feature of which was to separate religious and political authority into different castes (Braudel, 1994 [1987]: 217–21). Persian empires stretched to the Indus by 500 BC, and so did Alexander the Great's empire in the fourth century BC. The Romans established maritime trading posts in the subcontinent by the first century BC (Curtin, 1984: 99–103). Islamic incursions from the eighth century AD turned into a general invasion, and increasingly occupation, after the twelfth century. To the east, Southeast Asia contained no distinctive indigenous civilizations or powers capable of either threatening the subcontinent militarily or challenging it culturally.

India was centrally placed in the Eurasian trading system both as a producer of export goods (silk, spices, cotton, iron) and as an importer and trans-shipper of goods from both east and west. It was in the middle of the maritime Silk Roads, which from the fourth century BC began to link up the regional maritime trading systems of the Middle East, South Asia, Southeast Asia, and Northeast Asia (Paine, L., 2014: ch. 6). The Chinese were slow to go to sea in their own ships rather than in the ships of foreign merchants, and the first recorded Chinese ship to sail to India was in the second century AD (Jacq-Hergoualc'h, 2002: 264). Chinese Buddhists were making pilgrimages to India by the fifth century (Jacq-Hergoualc'h, 2002: 51-7; Hansen, 2012: loc. 4579). The maritime routes were much stimulated by the Tang/Abbasid imperial period starting in the seventh century (Chaudhuri, 1985: 34-62). By the ninth century AD, direct round trips by Muslim traders from the Gulf to Canton (Guangzhou), taking around eighteen months, had become common, though by the tenth century the pattern reverted to inter-regional trading, with India and Southeast Asia as intermediaries (Curtin, 1984: 106-8; Chaudhuri, 1985: 37-41). Indian polities, like China, were dominated by a continentalist perspective, taking little interest in the sea (Hodgson, 1993: 197; Risso, 1995: 40-1, 56-68). Therefore, like China, and also with one exception (the Chola empire, on which more below), classical India never developed sea power or more than local coastal shipping (Jacq-Hergoualc'h, 2002: 74, 95, 270, 279).

It was in this cultural, military, and economic crossroads that India's worldview emerged. Braudel (1994 [1987]: 226, 228) observes that Hinduism 'sought to embrace everything', it was 'more than a religion or a social system: it was the core of Indian civilization'. The Hindu caste system was a very powerful form of social hierarchy, providing significant forms of social and economic order that did not require political structures in order to maintain and reproduce themselves (Mann, 1986: 341-72). The overall Indian political order was consequently decentralized at birth and remained so despite interludes of strong imperial rule, which after the Mauryan and Gupta empires were mostly imposed by outsiders.

Thinking

There are three main strands of thinking about IR in India: Kautilya's *Arthashastra*, often associated with realism; *Dharma*, mostly coming out of Emperor Ashoka's Buddhism; and ideas about epistemology and ontology coming out of the Indian classics.

Kautilya's *Arthashastra*

The realist side of Indian thinking about IR is much the best known. This is because Kautilya's *Arthashastra* (The Science of Material Gain) was picked up by modern realists as a justification for the 'timelessness' of their thinking. The *Arthashastra* has aroused much debate over its authorship (single or joint), timing (when was it composed[3]), and intent (was the motive behind its composition religious or secular) (Shahi, 2020a: 1).

But the text undoubtedly contains much that resonates with realist thinking. Much of it is about the struggle for wealth, power, and pleasure; assumptions of inevitable conflict in human affairs; prudence in foreign (and domestic) policy; and understanding things as they are rather than as they should be (Liebig and Mishra, 2017: 5-6, 12-13). Interesting in this regard are two articles about the 'Hindu theory' of both the state and international relations by the Indian scholar Benoy Kumar Sarkar (1919, 1921) (Bayly, 2017). Sarkar was well acquainted with both Indian and Western thinking about the state and IR and, using the work of Indian thinkers such as Kautilya and Kamandaka, he went out of his way to argue that classical 'Hindu' thinking about the state and IR was virtually identical to the Western tradition of realism extending back to classical Greece, though much earlier than it. He saw the 'Mandala' doctrine as essentially about power politics, the permanency of war, and ruthless *realpolitik*, with peace only possible if one ruler can force all the other princes into submission. This idea

---

[3] The dating of the *Arthashastra*, rediscovered in 1905, is controversial. Some date it to fourth century BC, around the time of the Mauryan dynasty, while others date it to third century AD. An emerging consensus seems to reject fourth century BC and date the first written version to the middle of first century AD but drawing on sources from previous centuries. Michael Liebig and Saurabh Mishra (2017: 24-8) argue that Kautilya's work built on an earlier tradition of Arthashastras that are now lost. The text is also believed to have undergone revisions in later periods. According to Patrick Olivelle, a noted authority and translator of the *Arthashastra*, the text 'cannot be dated after the end of the 1st century AD, because in his chapter on coinage, he [Kautilya] is ignorant of gold coins which were in circulation during the Kushan period beginning around the end of the 1st century AD' (email, 5 April 2020, 12:31PM EST).

that peace could only be achieved with a universal empire was common to the CAPE era, but it was mainly a recipe for war in attempting to attain that (never reached) goal. Regarding the state, he saw 'Hindu' theory as very similar to Hobbes' theory, starting with a dim view of human nature (greedy and violent) and working out from the need to control the consequent anarchic state of nature to a Leviathan able to exercise firm coercive rule to enforce law and property rights.

Kautilya's overriding foreign policy aim was the unification of India while keeping something like balance-of-power relations with polities outside the subcontinent (Liebig and Mishra, 2017: 3–5; Mitra, 2017: 36). It is important to keep in mind that Kautilya's book, like those of Nizam al-Mulk (2002) and Ibn Khaldun (1969 [1370]) were written as handbooks of statecraft for the princes of CAPEs (Buzan and Lawson, forthcoming, ch. 4–6). As noted, such polities had both a much more open and fluid understanding and practice of territoriality, and a much less well-defined distinction between domestic and foreign policy, than Westphalian states. Whether they flourished or decayed depended heavily on the quality and competence of the prince. For such polities and their dynastic leaders, the idea of *l'etat c'est moi* was not far from the political reality.

The *Arthashastra* contains much advice on policies to conquer enemies, expand territory, and manage empire, including through such means as war, assassinations, spying, etc. The thoughts of Kautilya and Machiavelli share many similarities, but Kautilya pre-dates the latter by at least a millennium and a half and also makes the rulers more accountable for the happiness of the people. And it was Kautilya who developed one of the first systematic frameworks for thinking about foreign policy and international relations, his 'Mandala' ('circle of kings' or 'circle of states') theory (Liebig and Mishra, 2017: 9–10; Spruyt, 2020: 253–83).

The Mandala theory prescribes the position and policy of amity and enmity for an aspiring conqueror, an individual rather than a state. The countries surrounding the aspirant's territory are likely to be his enemies, whereas those surrounding the enemies' territory are likely to be his friends. But this is a dynamic model, dependent not just on geographic position. The varying incentives and sanctions pursued by the would-be conqueror, such as compensation, conciliation, divide and rule, and force, ultimately shape the loyalty and opposition of other states in the neighbourhood and beyond. To this end, Kautilya also prescribes a set of foreign policy measures to the ruler, including peace treaties, remaining passive, pre-emptively striking the enemy, and pursuing alliances with other rulers.

William McNeill (1965, 331–2) notes that Kautilya's *Arthashastra*, 'bears a strong imprint of Hellenistic ideas', especially the Greek notion of the 'supremacy of the state over all aspects of human activity'. However, he also concedes that the actual practice of the Mauryan administration was based on the pre-existing system developed in the Magadha state and 'although Chandragupta and his successors may have been dazzled by Hellenistic concepts of rulership, it was an indigenous Indian stratum that prevailed in the end'. Hence, this was probably a matter of Mauryan localization, rather than wholesale adoption, of some Greek ideas, although there is no firm evidence on this. It is possible that Alexander the Great's venture into the Indus region, which was apparently witnessed by the founder Chandragupta Maurya, might have influenced his thinking. But there is no definitive evidence for these presumptions, and some of these suppositions about Greek influence may be due to Helleno-centrism or the tendency of Western historians to attribute important political ideas and innovations to ancient Greece. There is more reason to suppose that ancient north India was influenced by Persian political and administrative ideas and practices, but again it was more a case of selective localization than outright borrowings from Persia.

Some scholars (e.g., Singh, 1993: 127) view the Mandala as a balance of power theory of international relations. Rejecting this, Roger Boesche (2003, 19–20) argues:

One does find this argument occasionally in Kautilya: 'In case the gains [of two allies of equal strength] are equal, there should be peace; if unequal, fight,' or, 'the conqueror should march if superior in strength, otherwise stay quiet.' Whereas these balance of power theorists suggest that a nation arm itself so that it can ensure peace, Kautilya wanted his king to arm the nation in order to find or create a weakness in the enemy and conquer, even to conquer the world, or at least the subcontinent of India.

Less well publicized aspects of Kautilya's political thought are his views on legitimacy and restraint. A good deal of the *Arthashastra* may seem to be about expansion and conquest, but he also recognizes the importance of virtue and pragmatism (Sharan, 1992, 206–7) and the need to ensure the support of the vanquished peoples. These anticipate the prudential side of realist thinking. For example, a passage in the *Arthashastra* illustrates this by saying:

Which enemy is to be marched against – a powerful enemy of wicked character or a powerless enemy of righteous character? The strong enemy of wicked character should be marched against, for when he is attacked, his subjects will not help him, but rather put him down or go to the side of the conqueror. (Kautilya, 1915)

But Deepshikha Shahi (2014: 72) argues that Kautilya goes beyond mere prudence: 'Moral considerations do enter into Kautilya's calculations. The eclectic interpretation of *Arthashastra* clearly demonstrates that the Vijigisu [an aspiring conqueror] is not merely motivated by the Realist ambition of power maximization[4] ... the actual power enhancement of Vijigisu requires a moral concern for the notion of justice and tolerance'. Thus, Kautilya advises that a would-be conqueror should expand their territory by seeking submission first

---

[4] We note, however, that 'power maximization' is a neo-realist claim; classical realism is more about prudence and does allow for some moral considerations (see Yan, 2019).

without waging a war of conquest. Once submission has been ensured and the flow of tribute established, it is not wise to displace the defeated ruler because they are likely to become a perpetual enemy of that state. If a ruler is not proving to be amenable to imperial rule, the conqueror should replace them with a relative without destroying the dynasty. Moreover, a conquering king should 'order the release of all prisoners and render help to the distressed, the helpless and the diseased' (*Arthashastra*, cited in Boesche, 2003: 143). This would reduce disaffection and the possibility of future revolt. There was a practical, power-political reason behind his humane approach, but it was humane nonetheless.

Much more research needs to be done to establish whether Mauryan emperors such as Chandragupta and Ashoka conquered territories and took away a lot of slaves like the Romans did or pursued a more indirect and possibly more humane approach, but there is a clear injunction in Kautilya's work to treat the conquered people justly. It was common practice in CAPEs from ancient Mesopotamia to the British empire to leave the local rulers in place, govern through them, extract taxes, and provide benefits in terms of trade, law, currency, and protection. As noted earlier, this enabled such empires to expand quickly at relatively low cost, though it also meant that they disintegrated quickly when the centre weakened.

In the West, Kautilya is usually compared with Machiavelli. Both advised the ruler on how to defeat enemies and expand territory. But Kautilya's *Arthashastra* does many other things, including offering the first known comprehensive definition of the state. *Arthashastra*'s *saptanga* (seven elements of the state) includes *Swami* (ruler), *Amatya* (minister), *Janapada* (which connotes both population and territory), *Durga* (fortress), *Kosha* (treasury), *Danda* (army, although the literal meaning of the word is punishment), and *Mitra* (alliances). Kautilya's work provides a more detailed account of the state and its institutions than that of Plato and Aristotle. As Ram Sharan Sharma (1996: 38) contends, 'Although Plato and Aristotle speculate on the origin of the state, they never define it as sharply and clearly as is the case with early Indian thinkers. In this sense, Kautilya furnishes us as full and complete a definition of the state as can be found in ancient times.'

Sbrata K. Mitra (2017: 41–2) makes the important point that the *Arthashastra* was not just relevant to its own time. He argues that the work has been continuously available and discussed throughout India's history and has become part of the subcontinent's collective memory or 'political habitus'. This gives it a parallel role in Indian thinking about IR to that enjoyed by Thucydides, Hobbes, and Machiavelli in the West; Confucius and Sun Tze in China, and Ibn Khaldun in the Islamic world.

Ashoka's *Dharma*

If Kautilya marked the highpoint of ancient realism and rationalism, the idealism and moral statecraft of ancient India was epitomized by Emperor Ashoka. Ashoka was the third ruler of the Mauryan dynasty.

In the later part of his rule, he embraced Buddhism, a religion that mainly focused on the individual and lacked much if any theory of the state or of world order in a political sense (Braudel, 1994 [1987]: 222–4). But Ashoka left a legacy of practice during his rule between 269 and 232 BC. After the Kalinga War, circa 261 BC, in which 100,000 died and 150,000 people were taken as prisoners, he converted to Buddhism and never waged war again. Instead, he pursued moral conquest and humanitarianism, called *Dharma* (*Dhamma* in Pali), or Law of Piety or righteousness. It signifies 'a sense of universality of affection for all people – an early form of humanitarianism which is not limited to war' (Draper, 1995). In a network of righteous relationships, 'no one was outside its ambit, not even Asoka or the Empress: censors were appointed to ensure that the Law of Piety was observed even in the latter's apartments in the Palace. The Law of Piety was a moral law, an imperial law, a law governing foreign relations and a way of life' (Draper, 1995).

Ashoka is referred to in Buddhist texts as a *chakravartin*. The Sanskrit term *chakravartin*,[5] notes Romila Thapar (2012: 184), implies 'a universal emperor whose dominions included the whole of Jambudvipa. His rule was just and his reign prosperous. He was so virtuous a king that he came to be regarded as having the power of divinity.' 'Jambudvipa' is an ancient name of India, which conceived the entire country as an island or 'dvipa'. There is a seeming conflict here between building an empire by conquest (a realist approach) and ruling by virtue. Many Chinese emperors kept on expanding their territory by force while at the same time claiming to rule by virtue. But in the case of Ashoka, he renounced further conquest only after his empire was firmly established. There is no record of further wars under his rule. Yet, he did not give up conquered territories either. Thapar (2012: 184) believes that while the term *chakravartin* might have existed earlier, it was fully developed only with the Mauryas, especially with Ashoka's reign. In any case, the term implies a combination of might and right as the basis of authority. In ancient India, the title was used sparingly to apply to those monarchs who had come to represent the highest principles expected of a ruler. This might include an ability for military conquest but also for non-violent authority.

The doctrine of *Dharma* is discerned from Ashoka's numerous inscriptions (Dhammika, 1993), as well as practice. Out of these, three aspects of the doctrine may be noted. The first is the relations between the ruler and the subjects. One of Ashoka's inscriptions reads: 'All men are my children. What I desire for my own children, and I desire their welfare and happiness both in this world and the next, that I desire for all

---

[5] One half of the word, 'chakra', translates into 'circle', while the other, 'vartin', means 'abiding in'. Therefore, the word as a whole is a reference to one who abides in the circle. The circle is symbolic of the disk of Vishnu, one of the three principal deities in the Hindu pantheon whose function is to maintain order in the world (the other two being Brahma, the creator, and Shiva, the destroyer).

men'. The second aspect concerned relations with neighbouring states, as stipulated in another inscription: 'The people of
the unconquered territories beyond the borders might think:
"What is the king's intentions towards us?" My only intention
is that they live without fear of me, that they may trust me and
that I may give them happiness, not sorrow' (Dhammika, 1993).
Third, King Ashoka can also be credited with an ancient doctrine of human rights. According to another inscription, 'While
being completely law-abiding, some people are imprisoned,
treated harshly and even killed without cause so that many
people suffer ... the judicial officers of the city may strive to
do their duty and that the people under them might not suffer
unjust imprisonment or harsh treatment' (Dhammika, 1993).
There is some gap between these pious statements carved on
stone and the actual practice of the Ashoka's state. While he did
not wage war after his brutal defeat of Kalinga, neither did he
set the Kalingas free.

Ontology and Epistemology

Modern political science and IR scholarship is deeply concerned about, and divided over, epistemological questions,
especially the relative importance of scientific/rationalist versus reflective or 'classical' methods. These questions are embedded in philosophy, including philosophy of science. India is
often seen in the West as the epitome of classical Eastern
knowledge, characterized by other-worldliness, one that is
beholden to mysticism and divine causation. However, there
is ample evidence of worldliness, secularism, and rationalism
in the Indian political and philosophical tradition. There are
aspects of Hindu Vedic philosophy which attribute causality to
natural forces such as fire (*Agni*), air (*Vayu*), and water (*Varuna*,
god of the ocean), even if these are worshipped as gods. As
S. Radhakrishnan, who was trained as a philosopher and
worked as an Oxford professor before becoming the second
president of independent India, put it, 'Religion, science, and
humanism were sisters in ancient India; they were allies in

Greece' (Radhakrishnan, 1940: 294). To the extent that the natural and the divine are deeply intertwined, it would be illogical to see ancient Indian philosophy as purely unscientific or 'other-worldly'. For example, Samkhya, one of the main schools of Hindu philosophy, which originated in the Vedic period and became a distinct philosophy perhaps around ninth–eighth century BC, 'contradicts divine origins of the universe and the tenets of supernatural religion by substituting evolution for creation'; it is 'essentially rational, anti-theistic, and intellectual', whose 'major concern is to explain the workings of nature through perceptual knowledge' (Singhal, 1993: 159; see also Larson, 1998). The Samkhya school holds that the primary constituents of the world, such as earth, water, fire, and air, were 'eternal' and 'the direction of the world was caused by the world itself' (Singhal, 1993: 157).

To sum up, like many ancient civilizations, the Indian civilization is an eclectic mix of reason and revelation, of science and superstition, and of worldliness and other-worldliness. At the very least, these divergent traditions have coexisted in India since antiquity, challenging the idea of a purely scientific approach to the study of the international. Patrick Thaddeus Jackson (2010: 193) argues that IR should not be seen as a science in the Newtonian sense. A variety of phenomena which are not technically part of the natural sciences can be accommodated within the epistemology of IR, but he draws the line when he declares that IR can only deal with this-worldly and not 'other-worldly phenomena'.[6]

But drawing such a line is questionable. There is emerging work (Bain, 2020) on the link between medieval Christian beliefs and the evolution of modern ideas of international order. In Islam, there is the doctrine of eternity of the world, which was a revival and expansion of an earlier Aristotelian doctrine, which challenges divine creation. This has been

---

[6] For Jackson (2010: 193), scientific knowledge has three indispensable 'constituent components': it must be systematic, it must be capable of taking (and one presumes tackling successfully) public criticism, and 'it must be intended to produce worldly knowledge'.

used to argue for secular, purposeful, human agency in creating international order. We could do the same for India at least, since it was in India that the debate about the natural versus divine causation of all things was most pronounced in the ancient world. This challenges the stereotype of India as mystical or other-worldly, where all things come from the divine. In India, Kautilya's secular ideas of statecraft, the anti-divine precepts of Samkhya philosophy, and even Ashoka's moral (but not religious) doctrine of *Dharma* (which does not mention god or Buddha, despite his reputation as a patron of Buddhism) make a powerful case that India offered a secular vision of world order, before the Romans and as much as the almost-contemporary Greeks.

The *Mahabharata,* one of India's epics, provides clues about statecraft, diplomacy, alliances, and negotiations in ancient India (Narlikar and Narlikar, 2014; Datta-Ray, 2015). Its plot revolves around the rivalry between the just and virtuous Pandava brothers and their cousins the Kauravas, whose greed far exceeds their sense of righteousness. The five Pandavas, the rightful heirs to the throne of Hastinapura, are tricked into exile by the Kauravas, who number a hundred siblings and are led by the unscrupulous eldest brother, Duryodhana. After completing their exile, the Pandavas return to claim the throne but are rebuffed. War ensues and ends in total defeat for the Kauravas. What led to the *Mahabharata* war? (Acharya, 2011). For an answer, we may turn to the 700-verse section of the *Mahabharata* known as *The Bhagavad Gita,* the bible of Hinduism. Just before going into battle, Arjuna, the leading warrior among the Pandava brothers, gets cold feet and does not want to fight for fear of killing his own relatives, the Kauravas. But the driver of his war chariot, Krishna, who is an incarnation of God Vishnu, tells him:

- You should fight because your cause is just as your family was cheated of their kingdom by the Kauravas (in a gambling match).

- If you do not fight your enemies, they will shame and conquer you. If you are proved to be a coward withdrawing from the battlefield your enemies will say you were weak.
- If you fight and win, you will achieve personal honour and status. You will then be considered a mighty warrior and conqueror and your honour and status will increase.
- If you fight and win, you will gain sovereignty and territory.
- Why worry about killing your own relatives? Killing does not mean anything. The soul is immortal. The soul is not going to die.

Out of the above five reasons, four are very rational. They reveal self-regarding motivation, comprising revenge, honour, independence, and territorial gain. Even justice as a motivation is linked to revenge, since Arjuna's family was cheated of its rightful claim to power. We can all relate to these motivations as rational and self-interested. This is what the writings on the causes of war tell you, and one can find them in any contemporary discussion of war and peace. The fifth one cannot be found there. What about the fifth reason, which holds that there is no need for Arjuna to worry about fighting and killing his relatives because their soul is immortal? Is the soul visible and provable? Does it mean IR must reject the *Mahabharata* as a text with no rational element? Most civilizations combine worldliness with other-worldliness. The West has no monopoly over rationality, the East has no monopoly over mysticism. Plato and Pythagoras believed in the soul, as much as did the mythical characters of the *Mahabharata*.

And as a contribution to both epistemology and ontology, it is from Buddhism that one gets the earliest social contract theory of the origin of the state (Thapar, 2002: 149–50). It includes an original state of harmony, decay, competition for satisfying basic needs to private property, disputes, need for law, and controlling authority. The elected authority (Great Elect) rule and maintain justice (Thapar, 2002: 149–50). Buddhist philosophy also values ideas about causality and change. The Doctrine of Emptiness (*Sunyata*) and 'dependent origination' (originating from the Indian Buddhist philosopher Nagarjuna from the second century AD) tells us that there is no such thing as a permanent reality, or that anything considered real is not absolute or permanent but is relative, conditional, and constantly evolving (Dalai Lama, 2005: 47, 66–7). Hence, 'causation implies contingency and dependence, while anything that inherently existed would be immutable and self-enclosed' (Nagao, 1991: 174–5). This combines rationality and relationality, and it invites comparison with today's constructivist IR theory (Wendt, 1992), which holds that conditions like peace, war, anarchy, etc., are not permanent or given but change over time.

Practice

Of the relevant practices on which an Indian IR might draw, two stand out: the *Mahajanapadas* as the pre-imperial political form of India and the peaceful spread of Indian culture to East and Southeast Asia.

The *Mahajanapadas*

The structure and worldview of the ancient Indian political order started differently than in China, not with a single dynasty like the Shang or a preeminent one, like Zhou, but with a number of small independent polities (*Mahajanapadas*).[7] Around 600 BC, sixteen *Mahajanapadas* existed. They were Kasi, Kosala, Anga, Magadha, Vajji, Malla, Chedi, Vatsa, Kuru, Panchala, Machcha, Surasena, Assaka, Avanti, Gandhara, and Kamboja. These *Mahajanapadas* continued for more than three centuries before the Mauryan empire, running contemporaneously with the

---

[7] The term *Mahajanapada* has three elements: *maha* means great, *jana* refers to people. While *pada* literally means foot in Sanskrit, it can be interpreted as place or realm. *Mahajanapada* thus means Great Realm. They were an enlargement in size and power of smaller realms, or simply *janapadas*. The latter had emerged after nomadic Indo-Aryan tribes from Central Asia had settled into a more sedentary agriculture-based way of life, developing small urban centres. After a period of conquest or voluntary merger among the smaller polities, the *Mahajanapadas* emerged.

better known Warring States period in China (475–221 BC). They were the seedbed for the revival of cities and high culture in India.

Some of these polities had hereditary rulers, while others had a republican form of government called a *Ganasangha* (literally 'assembly of people'). These, which included the Vrijii confederacy, Malla, Kuru, Panchala, and Kamboja, were not democracies but clan-based oligarchies which rejected Vedic ideals and Brahmanic rituals. Some of the dissenting philosophical and religious systems, including Jainism and Buddhism, emerged from founders who were from the republican polities. These *Ganasanghas* evoke the idea of an 'anarchic' inter-state system and have been compared to both Greek city-states, in terms of the 'republican' structure of both (Altekar, 2001: 113), as well as the Roman Republic (Basham, 2004: 97), for allowing greater participation of people than traditional monarchies. Some but not all Greek city-states allowed more direct citizen participation than the *Ganasanghas*, which nonetheless operated through an assembly, where the heads of families or heads of clans (in a confederacy) met to make decisions: 'The matter for discussion was placed before the assembly and debated, and if a unanimous decision could not be reached it was put to vote' (Thapar, 2002: 148).

The state system of ancient India could only be described as 'anarchic' inasmuch as a number of rival states 'each have a chance of gaining supremacy over the others'. Kautilya's *Arthashastra* thus described not the state of the Mauryan empire but the immediate period preceding it, that is, the period of the *Mahajanapadas* before the Mauryan empire emerged. Like the Warring States period in China, on which more in the next chapter, the period of the *Mahajanapadas* thus laid the practical foundations for what became India's version of realism. Moreover, republican states continued to coexist with and after Mauryan rule, at least until the Gupta empire. Some historians claim that these systems existed over much of India, including the south (Sastri, 1967: 173). And this was by no means exceptional in Indian history: 'the co-existence of various smaller rivalling kingdoms was much more typical for most

periods of Indian history than the rather exceptional phase
when the great empire completely dominated the political
scene' (Kulke and Rothermund, 1986: 63).

The relationships between these Indian states were governed
by warfare, alliance-making, and diplomacy. Some accounts
suggest a relationship of hostility among the republics, even
'a perpetual state of warfare' (Sharma, 1996: 122).
A *Mahajanapada* could be created by combining a number of
smaller *Janapadas*, either through conquest by a stronger one
among them or through voluntary confederation (as with the
Vrijii confederation). Amalgamation occurred through both
'conquest and encroachment' and a bipolar struggle for dominance ensued between the two most powerful states, Magadha
and Kosala (Kosambi, 1975: 154-5), as both tried to annex
smaller tribal states. While available Indian historical records
do not permit a confident generalization or comparison with
China's contemporaneous Warring States system, the tendency
in India was towards conquest and absorption of the weak by
the strong. Thus, in 322 BC, a century before China's unification under the Qin dynasty, most of the *Mahajanapada* polities
were conquered and absorbed by the Magadha, which under
the Mauryan rulers established India's first 'universal' empire.
In contemporary IR vocabulary, the Mauryan empire marked
India's transition from anarchy to universal empire. Hence
India might be Asia's first universal empire east of Persia. The
Mauryan empire might have affinities with the Achaemenid
Persian empire (McNeill, 1965: 331-2), the largest empire of
the ancient world, which as noted bordered the Mauryan
empire (the latter considered Western India to be a part of the
Persian empire).

Within the international relations of the subcontinent, India,
like most other civilizations of the ancient and classical world,
thus evolved an international system that oscillated between
anarchy and empire. In India's case, the balance was more
towards anarchy as the norm and empire as the periodic exception. But India also developed its own distinctive practices and
institutions, including pacific ways in which a ruler could

manage his empire but more importantly ways of spreading its culture that were largely detached from empire and coercion.

The Peaceful Spread of Indian Culture

Although the idea of *soft power* does not, with the possible exception of Ashoka's *Dharma*, feature much in Indian thinking about IR, a good case can be made that it certainly featured in India's practice. It is thus an available resource for Indian thinking about IR. India was known for both overland and maritime commerce through the Eurasian and maritime Silk Roads. The maritime dimension was consistent with India's location in the northern mid-point of the Indian Ocean trading network linking East Africa, the Mediterranean, the Red Sea, the Arabian Peninsula, and Persia to Southeast Asia and the China-centred East Asian region. This role and location provided the basis for the diffusion of Indian ideas, especially to Northeast and Southeast Asia. Buddhism travelled far and wide out of India, having a major impact in both Northeast and Southeast Asia. It did so mainly peacefully, travelling along overland trade routes. To a lesser extent, Hinduism did the same, but often the two religions travelled together and fused in practice. In places such as Cambodia, Indonesia and Thailand, China, and Japan both Buddhist and Hindu deities are worshipped in the same temple. Buddhism, indeed, is memorably described by Louis Schneider (1970: 75–7) as 'the export form of Hinduism'.

As described above, India was centrally placed in the Eurasian trading system and offers perhaps the best example in history of the peaceful diffusion of ideas. One might compare the 'Hellenization' (the spread of Greek ideas and institutions) in the Western Mediterranean and West Asia with what some historians call 'Indianization' (the spread of Indian, including Hindu–Buddhist, religious and political ideas and institutions) in Southeast Asia, Central Asia, and Northeast Asia (China, Korea, Japan). Hellenization was marked by conquest (Alexander in Egypt and Asia) or displacement of native peoples

(Greek City States in Sicily). Indianization was for the most part peacefully accomplished without such displacement. Hellenization was carried out by the Greeks and benefitted the Greek settlers, and it was for, by, and of the Greeks. Indianization was through voluntary initiative of local societies and rulers. It benefitted and legitimized local rulers and advanced local societies. It was for, by, and of the local societies. Hellenization often meant imposition of Greek culture, ideas, and institutions. Indianization often meant selective adaptation (rather than wholesale adoption) of Indian culture, ideas, and institutions by local societies in accordance with their prior beliefs, practices, and needs.

The spread of Hinduism and Buddhism did not just involve export of cultural ideas. It was also about political ideas. Hindu–Buddhist cosmological concepts, including identification of the ruler with Hindu gods such as Shiva and Vishnu, were used by Southeast Asian rulers to legitimize themselves before their subjects and expand their authority. In China, the Tang dynasty Emperor Wu Zetian (China's only female emperor), used Buddhist cosmology to consolidate her rule. Indian texts such as the *Arthashastra* and Code of Manu had been used in Southeast Asia in building its legal and political order. Spruyt (2020: 253–325), for example, documents the extensive influence of Hinduism, Buddhism, and the Mandala political principle in most Southeast Asian cultures. It would be an interesting research project to enquire as to whether or not Indianization had a more lasting impact on receiving societies than Hellenization (for a preliminary attempt comparing Hellenization and Indianization, see Acharya (2012, 60–70)), but it is useful to remind ourselves that Braudel (2001: 283) described the impact of Hellenization in the 'oriental soil' as 'no more than a layer, a poorly fitting mask'.

While the diffusion of Indian arts, culture, and political ideas peaked during the Gupta empire and was severely disrupted by the invasion of Islamic raiders in North India in the tenth century, Hindu–Buddhist ideas and their export continued to flourish in the south, spearheaded by regional powers such as the Chola empire from the tenth to thirteenth centuries AD and the Vijayanagar subsequently. The Chola empire was unusual for India in being maritime, extending its influence from its homeland on the east coast, down to Sri Lanka, and across the Bay of Bengal into Southeast Asia. Although the Cholas did not provide any major new political ideas, their imperial expansionist mode broke the mould of the otherwise pacific spread of Indian ideas to Southeast Asia. The Chola are considered responsible for the destruction of the Sri Vijayan kingdom, providing the one major exception to the rule of peaceful and largely commercial spread of Indian ideas.

Conclusion

Had IR developed in India, it would certainly have drawn on these classical sources of theory and practice. In that case, it would probably have evolved along similar lines to modern Western IR theory. Its main focus would have been on the states system, starting out from the dyad of realism/idealism. That distinction is not Western but is a general way of juxtaposing perspectives found in many civilizations: for example, Confucianism versus Legalism in China; Sufism versus Wahhabism in Islam. There is also the additional source of practice that might have been picked up by an emerging Indian IR: the peaceful spread of ideas or *soft power*. However, one has to be careful about the nature of the 'state' underpinning the approach to IR. It certainly would not have been the Westphalian one, nor the tributary system of China. As noted, India had city-states (*Mahajanapadas*) before the Mauryan empire, just as China had warring states before Qin. One can make a plausible case that if IR had been invented out of India or China, hierarchy, not anarchy in different forms, would be the main concern of IR theory. But India's might have been more pluralistic than China's, probably more similar to Europe before Westphalia. And there is a reason to believe that realism would have been the counterpoint, not idealism, since the ideals of Buddhism and Jainism, with their emphasis on non-violence, pre-dated the *realpolitik* of Kautilya, in a manner – as will be discussed in the next chapter – similar to the Zhou concept of *Tianxia*, pre-dating the *realpolitik* of Legalism.

Whether an IR born out of India would have downplayed or featured the cultural side of world order is an interesting question. Europe also had a major history of spreading ideas, particularly Christianity, socialism, nationalism, racism, and liberalism, though often done at the point of a sword. But Western IR theory has not featured this element, focusing more on interstate relations than on intercultural ones. There is also an important difference between India and Europe in this respect: while the Europeans exported ideas that were dominant within their own cultures, India's biggest success was Buddhism, which turned out to be fairly marginal within the wider Hindu, and later Islamic, sea of South Asia. The golden or classical age of Indian export of Buddhism occurred when Buddhism itself was a vital and widespread religion within India. Moreover, the co-mingling of Hinduism and Buddhism was commonplace. In Southeast Asia, for example, there were few purely Hindu states or Buddhist states but mainly Hindu–Buddhist states before the fifteenth century. In Cambodia, rulers switched between the two religions following a military defeat. Hinduism was thus a big part of Indian ideas export. However, both Hinduism as a political force and Buddhism as a cultural force severely weakened in India after the Islamic sultanate took hold of Delhi in the thirteenth century.

It may be true that India and China practised more intercultural relations than interstate ones, but this needs to be qualified. Europeans frequently used religion to justify conquest, alliances, and especially imperialism, ranging from papal blessings to the colonial voyages of Spanish and Portuguese missionaries accompanying, or closely following, colonial conquests and conversion becoming a primary mode of imperial administration and control.[8] Indian or Chinese theological history does

---

[8] As Niall Ferguson (2011: 142) notes, 'in the process of [European] empire-building [Christian] missionaries were nearly as important as merchants and military men'.

not show anything akin to Pope Alexander VI's papal bull dividing the world between the Spanish (who got the Americas) and the Portuguese (who got Africa and Asia), which was formalized in the 1494 Treaty of Tordesillas. India and China used religion more for symbolic legitimation at home than as a pretext for conquest. Unlike Christianity and Islam, Hinduism is not a proselytizing religion and therefore does not lend itself to religion as a basis for conquest.

At the risk of some oversimplification, in the East, cultural and political ideas from Buddhism and Hinduism were not imposed through force or even aggressive proselytization, with few exceptions, but spread through voluntary acculturation. So, while both West and East practised both interstate and intercultural relations, the Europeans did so more with force or through conquest (from Alexander's Hellenization to the colonial period). India and China did so more through voluntary acculturation; their ideas were borrowed more than imposed. This worked partly because of the prestige of India and China in neighbouring regions but also because of religious prohibitions against proselytization in Hinduism and the non-violent ethos traditions of Buddhism (whose main imperial figure, Ashoka, who initiated the export of Buddhism from India, became a pacifist).

This intercultural approach to IR is perhaps also contained in the Sanskrit phrase *vasudhaiva kutumbakam*, implying the whole world is one family. The continuity of this cultural way of thinking about IR in India is, like Kautilya's realist collective memory or 'political habitus', something actively handed down to the present. One example of this is the Indian writer and activist Rabindranath Tagore (1918), who was deeply concerned about the encounter between traditional culture on the one hand and modernity and Western power on the other, not just in India but in Asia as a whole. His perspective perhaps casts some useful light on the difference between India and China in the way they both composed themselves and faced the world. Tagore saw 'race' as India's eternal historic problem, by which he meant how a diversity of peoples and cultures could coexist peacefully together within the Indian subcontinent. In his view, India had addressed this quite successfully with a mixture of cultural and spiritual ideas, including the overarching caste system. This cultural halfway house between cosmopolitanism and nationalism was, he thought, existentially threatened by Western modernity and its promotion of a homogenous national state. Tagore saw Europe's (and increasingly Japan's) development as putting individualism before community and ruthlessly pursuing the competitive political and military mobilization of nations in pursuit of wealth and power. The Western concept of nation he saw as 'the aspect of a whole people as an organized power' (Tagore, 1918: 79). He saw nationalism in this sense as profoundly threatening to India, and indeed the whole of Asia, and advocated pan-Asian resistance to it. This idea of India as a set of culturally distinct nations bound together by a shared civilization looks more like Europe's erstwhile self-understanding as 'Christendom', or 'the great republic of Europe', and contrasts sharply with China's more homogenizing Han civilization.

Other modern Indian nationalist leaders, Gandhi and Nehru, would continue India's cosmopolitan tradition. Despite their staunch anti-colonial stance, both leaders rejected narrow nationalism. Gandhi's campaigns against racial discrimination in South Africa left a lasting legacy in shaping his internationalist outlook through his subsequent anti-British campaign in India. Moreover, the classical Indian approach to diffusion of ideas could be seen in the way these leaders approached ideology. Nehru, who went on to become India's first prime minister, used his office to practise a more active internationalism and promotion of the idea and practice of 'peaceful coexistence', which could be especially seen in his leadership role in pan-Asianism, the Bandung Asia–Africa Conference of 1955 and the Non-Alignment Movement.

4 CHINA

Introduction

Like India, China, and indeed all agrarian civilizations, fluctuated from empire to fragmentation and back again. But compared with India, China developed a much more hierarchical
political and interstate system. Even though India had its expo-
nent of universal empire in Kautilya, it never developed anything like China's theoretical and practical obsession with
hierarchy and unity. China's principle of social order, though
rooted in family, was, in contrast to Hinduism's mainly social
order, both social and political. In China, there was always
a presumption that when an existing dynasty became too
weak to maintain unity, a new one would arise to claim the
Mandate of Heaven and pull the country back together again
after a period of division.

Until the nineteenth century, China was relatively lightly
connected to the other sedentary civilizations of Eurasia, and
during its long history was consequently able to develop, and
maintain for millennia, a distinctive theory and practice of
world order. Both China and Europe were at the ends of the
Eurasian system, which made them relatively detached from
the other major centres of civilization. Ancient Greece and
Rome were in close touch with other civilizations in the
Middle East, which were in turn in direct touch with South
Asia. Medieval Europe was a civilizational backwater, though it
was deeply influenced by having been part of the Roman Empire
for several centuries. On the basis of its Roman-Christian legacy,
Europe began a long and defining military encounter with
Islamic civilization from the eighth century AD. China, however,
had only arms-length relay trading and cultural contact with
other Eurasian civilizations through the Silk Roads. China was

effectively penetrated by the diffusion of Buddhism over many
centuries. But in terms of trade and commerce, apart from the
early fifteenth-century voyages of Zheng He, few Chinese ships
ventured beyond the South China Sea. Trade was mostly carried
by foreign ships, and by the ninth century AD there is evidence
from tax records that more than 100,000 Muslims, Christians,
Jews, and Persians were living in the commercial settlements of
Canton (Chaudhuri, 1985: 51; Jacq-Hergoualc'h, 2002: 265). The
Silk Roads were mainly relay trade, where goods moved through
many local trading points. China's local military challenge came
mainly from the pastoralist, nomadic steppe barbarians to the
north, who the Chinese saw as culturally inferior no matter that
they could often defeat China militarily.

Before its unification in 221 BC, China was not in much
contact with outsiders and evolved mainly as a self-contained
world order which fluctuated between various degrees of unity
and fragmentation. Much of classical Chinese thinking about
world order, including Legalism and Confucianism, was
formed during this time when China itself was fragmented
into multiple, and often warring, states. After 221 BC, unity
was the dominant theme within China, though periodically
interrupted by invasions from the peoples of the steppe and
sometimes long transitional periods of fragmentation when
one dynasty was falling and another rising or several dynasties
existed simultaneously. As elsewhere in Eurasia, China was not
infrequently ruled by steppe dynasties; these were mainly
Manchu and Mongol, whereas Turkic dynasties tended to dominate in South and West Asia.

After unification, China also became engaged in varying
degrees with the wider world around it, with the Silk Roads
under the Han dynasty becoming a transmission belt for ideas,
goods, and diseases across Eurasia. Post-unification, China was
therefore both engaged as a player in a world order that
extended beyond itself and, sometimes, temporarily reverted
to being a fragmented system in its own right (most recently
between 1911 and 1949 with the warlord period and the civil
war). If we compare China's history and political theory about

world order with Europe's in this respect, they come out as near opposites. In China, the principle of unity was normatively dominant from an early point, though in practice the system suffered periodic breakdowns and fragmentations. In Europe, the principle of unity, though always present, was relatively weak normatively, despite having the compelling, and much admired, image of Rome behind it. Individual polities and dynasties might aspire to bring the continent under their rule, but in practice and in theory the desire for independence and self-government remained strong enough to prevent that outcome. The balance of power idea triumphed, and no attempt to form a durable European empire succeeded.[1]

This duality of China as both an international system and civilization in itself and a player in a wider international system has to be kept in mind when trying to understand the Chinese/Confucian view of world order. Edward Luttwak (2012: 260) takes this duality very seriously in strategic terms, seeing in China:

> *a deeply rooted strategic culture that is both intellectually seductive and truly dysfunctional. Its harmful consequences have marked the historical experiences of the Han nation, supremely accomplished in generating wealth and culture from earth and water by hard work and wonderful skill, but exceptionally autistic in relating to the non-Han, and therefore unsuccessful in contending with them whether by diplomacy or by force. Nor is this culture at all appropriate for the fluid conduct of inter-state relations among formal equals, as opposed to the management of a China-centred tributary system.*

---

[1] The operation of the balance of power against hegemony in Europe was mainly what Richard Little (2006, 2007) calls *adversarial*, driven by the responses of states and empires to what they perceived as threats to their independence. Not until the nineteenth century did *associational* balancing emerge, where the balance of power becomes a generally accepted principle and an institution of international society.

This unique insulation from direct military and political encounters with other settled agrarian civilizations perhaps goes some way to explaining the particular and distinctive form and character of Chinese thinking and practice about world order and international relations. Whereas Western thinking and practice were eventually drawn towards sovereignty, territoriality, international anarchy, war, and international society, Chinese theory and practice were drawn towards hierarchy, *Tianxia* (all under heaven), and the Mandate of Heaven, which combined to form the tribute system of relations. In the Chinese system, war, diplomacy, and trade all embodied quite different practices and understandings from those either in India or in the West. What is now called soft power played a much larger and more political role in the Chinese system than it did for India, where the diffusion of Indian culture and religion was largely separate from the state. It is common to note that China's relations with its civilized neighbours to the east (Korea and Japan) and south (Vietnam) were relatively peaceful and that its culture spread much more by acceptance than by imposition (Kang, 2010; Katzenstein, 2010: 34–5). That said, China's relations with its nomadic neighbours to the north were much more warlike (Kang, 2010: 112), and its internal politics periodically descended into extensive violence and power politics during dynastic transitions. Victoria Tin-bor Hui (2005), for example, tells a graphic story of ruthless power politics in the unification of China under the Qin dynasty, and China's history contains many turbulent and violent transitions between dynasties. Yasuaki Onuma (2000: 11–18) argues that China's insistent claim to superior status over all others, even if that claim could not always be enforced, prevented the emergence of thinking about international law within the Chinese sphere. China's claim to be the 'Middle Kingdom' was an assertion of cultural as much as material superiority, and Chinese practice and thinking often do not fit all that comfortably with Western concepts such as great powers, empire, and suzerainty.

Thinking

Yuri Pines (2012: 1–43, 162–70) argues that China's history generated a different view of politics and world order from that which unfolded in the modern West. He focuses particularly on the extremely violent experience of the Warring States period (453–221 BC) that led up to the unification of China, interpreting this as being so traumatic that it instilled in Chinese culture a permanent fear of the dispersal or separation of power. The Warring States period and the turbulent Spring and Autumn period (771–476 BC) that preceded it were the golden age of Chinese philosophy and political theory, and the trauma of these times drove many of these thinkers, Confucius most notably, to search for arrangements and practices that would prevent any repetition of it. Thus, whereas the West eventually learned the lesson that political pluralism both at home (democracy, separation of powers) and abroad (an anarchical international society based on separated sovereignty and territoriality and an international society of states) was to be desired, China came to the opposite conclusion. The lesson of the Warring States period, and of many other periods of disunity in Chinese history, was that political pluralism was a recipe for a ruthless round of fighting and disorder that would last until someone could once again reunify the country and accept the Mandate of Heaven to reign over all. Hierarchy in all relations and unity at home were thus China's default political preference, and anarchic separation of powers its nightmare. Hierarchy was a system of symbolic order. At times it came close to empire, especially within China, and sometimes in its relations with Vietnam and the steppe nomads. But in many of its external relations, it allowed too much local sovereignty to fit comfortably into the concept of empire as normally understood.

Pines' interpretation is, of course, a heroic simplification of a much more complicated reality. Chinese philosophy and political theory does not begin and end with Confucius but is a very deep, rich, and varied resource, influenced among other things by Buddhism and Daoism. It notably includes Legalism, an equally long tradition of Chinese thinking, running alongside Confucianism and interacting with it, which has some similarities to Western Realism/power politics. Legalism advocates the construction of both a strong state and a strong power (Pines, 2018). First formulated by Shang Yang and later by Hanfeizi, both philosopher-politicians, Legalism focuses on domestic rule but also has clear implications for interstate relations and world order. It holds that in order to conquer or defeat enemies and to regulate the 'all under heaven', a ruler must control its own people first. To quote the most important Legalist text, *The Book of Lord Shang,* 'In the past, those who were able to regulate All-under-Heaven first had to regulate their own people; those who were able to overcome the enemy had first to overcome their own people'. And the way to achieve this was through strict laws backed by harsh punishment. 'When the people are weak, the state is strong; hence the state that possesses the Way devotes itself to weakening the people' (cited in Pines, 2018).

Hui (2005) observes the extreme ruthlessness of state-strengthening to overthrow the balance of power system during the Warring States period and its influence on the Qin dynasty (221–206 BC) that first unified China. The Qin dynasty was short-lived, and Confucian and Daoist thinking was revived during the next major Chinese dynasty, the Han, who also introduced Buddhism into China, creating a plurality of political and social thought. Nonetheless, the political and administrative legacies of the Qin, especially the creation of a centralized professional bureaucracy, created a durable impetus in China's political system for strong and authoritarian rule. Indeed, an echo of Legalism can be found in current Chinese leader Xi Jinping, who is widely seen as creating the most authoritarian Chinese regime since Mao and who has cited Hanfeizi to justify the need for a country to have strong leaders upholding the law (rule *by* law, rather than rule *of* law). Thus, Xi quotes the following words of Hanfeizi: 'No country is permanently strong, nor is any country permanently weak. If those who impose The Law are strong, the country will be strong; if they are weak, the country will be weak' (Buckley, 2014; Zha, 2020).

In the case of Chinese thinking about world order, there is again the difficulty in disentangling the domestic from the international. Territoriality, and with it the distinction between inside and outside, is much blurrier than it is in the European tradition. China was, in the centuries before the Qin unification, both an international system and civilization in its own right, while later becoming a unified player in a wider international system with non-Chinese polities. But in China's case it also concerns the universalist aspects of Chinese thinking about world order. The Chinese/Confucian view of world order had three distinctive and intertwined components: a strong sense of *hierarchy* as the preferred social order; a universal sense of space/territory (*Tianxia* – all under heaven); and the idea of the Mandate of Heaven linking rulers and people. There are two additional ideas rooted in traditional Chinese culture that played into how the tribute system worked: *relationalism* and *face*. We are fortunate in having contemporary Chinese IR scholars who have made sustained attempts both to recover classical Chinese thinking about IR and to relate it to both contemporary (Western) IR theory and current Chinese foreign policy (e.g., Zhao, T., 2006, 2009, 2015; Qin, 2011, 2016, 2018; Yan, 2011, 2019). These five ideas combined to create the practice of the so-called tribute system, which defined how the Middle Kingdom related to those outside the Chinese cultural sphere.

Hierarchy

A good case can be made that thinking of social relations in hierarchical terms is a particularly strong and intrinsic feature of Confucian cultures, rooted deeply in an embedded philosophical tradition (Braudel, 1994 [1987]: 178–9). The basic Confucian model is rooted in a hierarchical family structure similar to that in many traditional agrarian civilizations in which fathers, brothers, sons, wives, etc., stand in status relations of dominant/inferior to each other, and these relationships are mediated by the degree of intimacy/distance (Shih, 1990: 39–46; Hwang, 2011: 109–10, 199). This kind of hierarchy is of course not unique. Most pre-modern agrarian societies, including in Europe, also had strong class ranking, patriarchy, and dynastic political legitimation.

Some literature supports the view that this way of thinking still applies in modern foreign policy terms, with Confucian cultures being more inclined to hierarchy and bandwagoning than to sovereign equality and balance of power (Fairbank, 1968; Huntington, 1996; Kang, 2003, 2003–4, 2005; Kissinger, 2011: 1–3; Harris, 2014: locs. 362–74. For a critique, see Acharya, 2003–4). Traditionally in East Asia, Confucianism operated mainly on the basis of a hierarchy rooted in the existence of a central culture, or more accurately, civilization: the Middle Kingdom as the apex of a cultural, political, and economic order. Material power was of course relevant to establishing and maintaining hierarchical relations but was not its main foundation (Zhang, Y., 2001; Suzuki, 2009: 34–55; Zhang, F., 2009, 2014; Zhang and Buzan, 2012). Both Western and Chinese scholars emphasize the ongoing importance of hierarchy in China's worldview. Stuart Harris (2014: locs. 362–74, 1289) notes that 'China sees the world in a different way than countries in the West, for various reasons, but mostly because of the Confucian belief in hierarchy'. Chih-yu Shih (1990:118–22), echoing Luttwak, argues that China remains in the grip of Confucian hierarchical relationalism and has failed to develop separate norms for dealing with interstate relations. This interpretation certainly fits both with China's keenness to deny equal status to Japan (Shi, 2007: 217–18; Odgaard, 2012: 169–77; Goh, 2013: 221; King, 2014; Dreyer, 2016: 360) and with its undiplomatic assertions in Southeast Asia about big versus small countries. In Confucian thinking, social harmony rests on the precondition of stable hierarchy. As Shih (1990: 40) puts it, 'The system is harmonious as long as everyone in his role behaves as the role requires'.

Jack Gray (2002: 18-19) nicely captures the traditional Confucian approach to maintaining social order:

> *The object of that culture was the maintenance of peace and stability in an agrarian society, in which change was neither sought nor anticipated. The highest value recognized in China was social harmony. The method by which the Chinese sought to realize this value was the control of conflict by the imposition of hierarchically organized authority.*

In this formulation, the link between hierarchy and harmony is almost absolute. As William Callahan (2009) rightly notes, the inseparability of harmony and hierarchy in Confucian thought imparts a worryingly imperial implication to China's current discourse about harmony. China's official foreign policy rhetoric has a lot to say about harmonious relations and 'win–win' but is generally silent or evasive about the hierarchical assumption that lies behind it. China seems to feel surprisingly comfortable sustaining the contradiction between its manifest interest in regaining primacy in Asia on the one hand and enthusiastically embracing the Westphalian principles of sovereignty and non-intervention on the other (more on China's ability to sustain contradictions in Chapter 6).

The linkage of hierarchy and empire, and the fears associated with it, have, however, to be mediated by differences in Western and Chinese conceptions of hierarchy. The Western conception tends to be associated with relations of dominance and extraction that were typical of Western empires. The Chinese conception, with its roots in Confucian family relations, is more reciprocal. The dominant side has the right to expect fealty and loyalty from the subordinate one but in return has clear obligations. Thus, as many have observed, the tribute system often did not work as a mechanism of extraction but rather benefitted the subordinate side materially. The balance of rights and duties in Confucian hierarchies gives the concept a distinctly different form, both morally and practically, from Western conceptions and destabilizes any too-easy conflation of hierarchy and empire. The tribute system was certainly paternalistic but perhaps fell somewhere between empire and hegemony and took a different form from empires elsewhere in Eurasia. By comparison, only quite late in Western imperialism did the paternalistic idea of the 'civilizing mission' obtain much traction: for those in the vanguard of both modernity and imperialism to bring the colonized peoples up to the 'standard of civilization'.

Tianxia

Tianxia (all under heaven) is a concept that goes back to the Zhou dynasty of China (beginning in eleventh century BC). It literally means the earth or all lands under the sky. The *Tianxia* system was designed by the Zhou, who had seized power from the Shang but soon found themselves surrounded by other, rising powers who were both numerically and materially superior, including the Shang whom the Zhou had displaced. Hence the Zhou approach represented an 'unusual and systematic innovation' that depended not on 'rule by force' but on legitimizing principles such as the Mandate of Heaven (to be discussed shortly) and 'a net-like world system that would create interdependence among all nations and guarantee the shared goods and benefits that were attractive to every nation in the network, therefore discouraging them from refusing or betraying the world system of *tianxia*' (Zhao, T., 2014: 128–9).

Tianxia has been applied by Chinese scholars (especially Zhao, T., 2006, 2009, 2015) to understand contemporary world order. In this view, *Tianxia* rejects the Westphalian model and blames it for problems of conflict and state failure. Instead, it sees the highest unit as the 'world', not the 'state'. *Tianxia* effectively sees the world as a single political space, a vision antithetical to the territoriality, borders, and inside/outside preoccupations of Western IR. As Tingyang Zhao puts it, 'The concept of tianxia means a world system that takes the world as a political actor or an order of coexistence that takes the world... as a political unit.' (Zhao, T., 2015: 2). When combined with hierarchy, *Tianxia* makes the traditional Chinese view of world order effectively a universal one by downgrading the significance of boundaries. Kissinger (2011: 357) notes that in the Chinese tradition of thinking about the world, the emperor notionally ruled all under heaven, a perspective that did not allow a strong distinction between home and abroad, or, in IR parlance, inside/outside.

Moreover, Zhao insists on the universal contemporary appeal of *Tianxia*: 'tianxia is not a special concept about China, but a concept about the world' (Zhao, T., 2015: 2). By taking as the highest unit of international relations the 'world' and not the nation-state, *Tianxia* expands the concept of international politics 'by introducing the dimension of global politics' (Zhao, T., 2015: 31). While the 'tianxia system of the Zhou Dynasty disappeared a long time ago ... today the concept of tianxia becomes the imagination about the future world.' (Zhao, T., 2015: 2). And he sees *Tianxia* as a prescription against modern anarchy disorder: 'Tianxia should be so established to be a world system based upon the ontology of coexistence by means of relational rationality, which gives the priority to the *minimization of mutual hostility over the maximization of exclusive interest*, in contrast to the individual rationality which gives the priority to the maximization of self-interest ... the impartial will of the heaven is above the partial preferences of human minds.' (Zhao, T., 2014: 1–2; emphasis original). This formulation is too open and ambiguous to be an obvious fit with Western IR concepts. The references to 'the ontology of coexistence' seem to rule out both world government and universal empire. It might fit more closely with the English School idea of a solidarist international society (i.e., one built on a logic of cooperation, not just coexistence), but there is a top-down element in it – 'the will of heaven' – that has no place in English School thinking.

For China, becoming a modern sovereign state legally equal to others was a major loss of status compared to its Middle Kingdom position in the *Tianxia* system. *Tianxia* is a tricky concept for China to deploy in the contemporary world. It can be useful as an idealist framing for thinking about the problems of humankind and the planet as a whole. It might, for example, be a way of framing global shared threats such as climate change, pandemics, and terrorism. But to the extent that it is linked with hierarchy, it threatens fundamentally the now widely and deeply accepted territorially bounded sovereign equality of the Westphalian international system/society. As such, it has been criticized for being politically motivated, as a theoretical justification for China's ruling elite (Zhao, S., 2017). It might, however, open a new perspective on how to think about the international system/society and the principles of world order.

The Mandate of Heaven

The Mandate of Heaven is also a concept from the Zhou dynasty (1026–256 BC). The ruler, the Son of Heaven, receives the right to rule from heaven (from Tian, who was the main god of the Zhou). If the ruler was not wise and just and ignored the welfare of the people, heaven would send warnings in the form of a natural disaster, an eclipse, or a peasant rebellion. If the ruler did not change his way, heaven would withdraw its mandate and his right to rule. The Mandate of Heaven can therefore be understood as a kind of performance legitimacy and in that sense is still very visible in Chinese politics today. The Mandate of Heaven was used by the Zhou dynasty founder, Wu, to justify the overthrow of the Shang dynasty's last ruler, Di Xin. The Mandate of Heaven was a double-edged sword. Rulers could use it to suppress any rebellion as an act against the will of the heaven. But it could also be used to justify rebellion against the ruler on the pretext that he was cruel and unjust. If the rebellion succeeded, it could be presented as evidence that the ruler had lost the mandate. Whichever side succeeded could claim the mandate. As Pines (2012: 134–40) perceptively observes, the Mandate of Heaven allowed *rebellions* but not *revolutions*. The point of rebellions was to replace leaders who had lost the mandate, not to replace the system itself. The role of the leader was crucial to the whole two-way formula of harmony-in-hierarchy. In return for the respect and obedience of the followers, leaders had to show *ren* (concern, kindness, forgiveness, love, wisdom, moral purity, and leadership) and be 'an unambiguous symbol of high moral spirit'. Although the hierarchical order forbids revolution, it sanctions the overthrow of leaderships that no longer display *ren*, seeing that overthrow as a return to normality (Shih, 1990: 40–1, 57).

One can perhaps understand the work of Yan Xuetong (2011, 2019), one of China's leading realist theorists of IR, in the light of the Mandate of Heaven. Particularly in his 2019 book, Yan puts a lot of emphasis on the quality of leadership as a crucial factor for great powers, both established and rising, though especially for the latter. Yan recovers from classical Chinese political theory and practice the ideas of 'the kingly way' and 'humane authority'. These ideas resonate with Shih's (1990) discussion noted above about the importance of *ren* to the viability of the whole 'harmony-in-hierarchy' formula. With echoes of Plato's philosopher-kings, wise and humane leaders become the key to squaring the circle of hierarchy, *Tianxia*, and the Mandate of Heaven, possibly even for modern times.

Epistemology–Relationality

China's classical political ideas are perhaps more secular than India's, although the latter, as we have seen, has powerful secular traditions, including Kautilya and Samkhya. Perhaps the most distinctive aspect of classical Chinese epistemology is *zhongyong* dialectics, which has been introduced to IR theory by Qin Yaqing (2018). Unlike the Hegelian concepts of thesis and antithesis ending in synthesis, the two ends in Chinese dialectics are contradictory but non-conflictual and mutually inclusive to start with. This scheme is based on the well-known yin/yang symbol in Chinese philosophy: the *yin* and the *yang* of a complementary and co-evolutionary process, where each always contains an element of the other and the balance between them shifts according to circumstance (see Figure 4.1).

The point of Hegelian dialectics is to resolve contradictions and start again from a new place. The point of

Figure 4.1 Yin and yang in Chinese zhongyong dialectics

zhongyong dialectics is to manage contradictions that are seen as permanent. Achieving harmony in the presence of contradiction is the essence of Chinese dialectics. Drawing on the epistemology of Chinese *zhongyong* dialectics, Qin argues that instead of rational calculations of self-interest and need, states and non-state actors alike often base their actions on relationships. It is relationships that make the world go around. Such a theoretical framework presents an alternative way of conceptualizing IR or allows us to see the world from a different perspective, including rethinking the relationship between power and governance, and allows for a more fruitful comparative study of international systems.

In contrast to Hegelian thinking, Chinese *zhongyong* (*yin* and *yang*) dialectics stresses a 'both–and' rather than an 'either–or' way of thinking and rejects the dichotomous Hegelian 'thesis' and 'anti-thesis' in favour of 'co-theses' (Qin, 2018: xvii). Whereas the Hegelian approach stresses individual rationality, the Chinese notion represents relational rationality. As he puts it, 'while the Hegelian tradition tries to diagnose the key contradiction, which is key to crumpling the old and creating a new synthesis', the '*zhongyong* dialectics always tries to find the appropriate middle where the common ground lies' (Qin, 2018: xvii).

Conflict exists but does not have any ontological status (Qin, 2018: xvii).

In sum, *zhongyong* dialectics agrees with Hegelian dialectics in that both understand things as consisting of polarities and their developments through the interaction of such polarities. But it differs from Hegelian dialectics in that *zhongyong* dialectics interprets the basic state of the relationship between the two polarities as capable of being harmonized if the right middle ground can be found, while Hegelian dialectics sees conflict as the essential nature of the polarization. The difference is fundamental (Qin, 2018: xvii). In contrast with the West, China (and Japan) lean more towards collectivism than individualism in their social practices (Qin, 2011: 127; Harris, 2014: loc.1379), which links to the disposition towards hierarchical relations. But Qin dismisses the commonly held view that Confucianism or traditional Chinese culture generally 'values collectivity at the expense of individuality'. Instead, it values both. Still, Qin (2011, 2018) argues that there are profound differences between Western rationalism and Eastern relationalism as approaches to social relations and that these differences significantly affect how diplomacy is conducted and international society managed. Rationalism risks reducing all relationships to mere individualist calculation, devoid of morality, trust, or the dynamics of personal relations. Relationalism is much more about trust in the process of interpersonal relations within a collectivist social framing. Seen from the prism of Confucianism, relationality 'holds that self-existence, self-identity, and self-interest are all related to other-existence, other-identity, and other interest' (Qin, 2018: xii). It is noteworthy that, among IR theories familiar in the West, Constructivism makes somewhat similar arguments, albeit mostly without either the normative content or the specific cultural rooting.

Qin does not say that Eastern relationality is superior to Western rationality. His point rather is that rationality – so often privileged in Western IR – without relationality fails to capture and explain a good deal of international relations.

Qin's theory appears to make a tight distinction between the West and China, sometimes openly, sometimes implicitly. Yet, the West also has middle-ground concepts, such as international society, that might resonate with Chinese ideas of harmony and the positive notion of power and inclusiveness. In highlighting the distinction between positive and negative dimensions of power, Qin (2018: xviii) implies that the West pays more attention to the negative dimension (power against), China more to the positive dimension (power with). But the West also has positive notions of power. Hence Qin's contribution is to shift the emphasis onto the positive notion of power, not to reject the negative notion. This also suggests Qin is trying to broaden our understanding of the relationship between power and IR. Moreover, Qin argues that the salience of relationality is universal, rather than being a unique attribute of Chinese or Asian societies. Western IR theories have not paid sufficient attention to relationality, which, like Constructivism, emphasizes process.

Qin makes a good case for the fact that, as in the *yin/yang* framing of Chinese dialectics, both rationalism and relationalism are present in Eastern as well as Western IR and practice. He argues that they overlap enough to be combined and that this needs to be done if diplomacy in a more multicultural, less West-centric international society is going to work. The key difference is that in the East relationalism comes first, while in the West, rationalism is the dominant logic. This offers useful ground for a meeting of minds if each side can recognize and acknowledge aspects of itself that are found more strongly in the other. One implication of Qin's argument is that China, Japan, and Korea should have more in common with each other in this respect than any of them has with Western countries. Their relations should be less subject to misunderstanding but perhaps more vulnerable to the narcissism of small differences (see Buzan and Goh, 2020: ch. 1), especially in relation to 'face', which is closely tied to both hierarchy and relationalism.

Face

'Face' is a cultural feature common to Confucian societies and shapes social interactions in ways quite different from those within Western culture (Tudor, 2012: 42–52; Moore, 2014). Face is a complex concept, relating partly to material accomplishments and positional status and partly to one's moral standing in one's community (Hu, 1944; Hwang, 2011: 266–81). David Yau-fai Ho (1976: 883) defines face as:

> *the respectability and/or deference which a person can claim for himself from others, by virtue of the relative position he occupies in his social network and the degree to which he is judged to have functioned adequately in that position as well as acceptably in his general conduct; the face extended to a person by others is a function of the degree of congruence between judgments of his total condition in life, including his actions as well as those of people closely associated with him, and the social expectations that others have placed upon him. In terms of two interacting parties, face is the reciprocated compliance, respect and/or deference that each party expects from, and extends to, the other party.*

Ho (1976: 883, 867, 873) also notes a 'Chinese orientation, which places the accent on the reciprocity of obligations, dependence and esteem protection'. In this sense, face is a more complex sociological formulation than mere esteem/ image/externalities, entailing roles, responsibilities, and mutualities. In this collectivist context, 'losing face is a serious matter which will, in varying degrees, affect one's ability to function effectively in society'. In the sense that life is meaningless without a legitimate social existence, not just social standing or position, 'face can be more important than life itself'. Shih (1990: 16–37) sets up a two-level model of face: the individual level refers to people searching 'for self-identities to satisfy their desire to confirm the meaning of life' (36), while 'national face' is about 'the continued meaningful existence of the whole to which the individual self belongs' (29).

Some Western authors take face seriously as a core feature of Northeast Asia's international relations, both historical and contemporary. For instance, S. C. M. Paine (2003: 257, 306, 349–51; see also Dreyer, 2016: 50) sees face as explaining a lot about the conduct of the Sino-Japanese war of 1894–5 and its ongoing importance in Sino-Japanese relations. For Peter Hays Gries (2004: loc. 223–55) face is both individual and collective, always social, and promotes self-justifying behaviour and self-serving interpretations of history. He gives extensive documentation of how China has sought to construct itself as superior to both the United States and Japan, gaining face for itself and taking it away from the other two. He shows how this interplay of nationalist rhetoric between China on the one hand and the United States and Japan on the other serves to construct China's nationalism and identity. David Shambaugh (2013: 55–9) agrees, arguing that China displays a huge amount of 'face diplomacy' to bolster the country's image in general and that of the Chinese Communist Party (CCP) and its leader in particular. Gregory Moore (2014) shows how face plays differently and often in contradictory ways in how governments in Northeast Asia relate to their domestic constituencies on the one hand and their neighbours on the other.

These themes resonate very strongly with Qin's (2011) analysis, which also emphasizes trust, reciprocity, and collectivist, hierarchical societies. Face and Asian relationalism seem to be closely linked, either as different ways of talking about the same thing or with face as a particular feature of relationalism in Confucian societies. Face is unquestionably an important and very longstanding feature of Northeast Asian cultures and is therefore almost certainly a key element in diplomatic relations both within the region and between the Northeast Asian states and the rest of the world. Shih (1990: 138–47, 189) argues that concern about face has a deep influence on Chinese diplomacy and that statesmen generally have a strong linkage to the 'national face'. This concept has not yet received either the amount or depth of attention it deserves in the IR literature. Both modern and classical international relations within the zone of Confucian civilization cannot be understood without it, and neither can the diplomacy of a rising China towards the rest of the world.

Practice

At some risk of oversimplification, classical China's practice of international relations can be divided into two parts: when it was a unified polity interacting with neighbours and when it was fragmented, and therefore a kind of international system in itself. When China was unified, especially from the Han dynasty (202 BC) onwards, its international relations largely took the form of the so-called tribute system, which Yongjin Zhang (2001: 56–8) among others depicts as the key institution of China's world order. When China was fragmented, it often looked like an extreme form of power politics, in which the contesting polities struggled ruthlessly among themselves to rebuild a centralized order. Neighbouring polities easily got involved in this process, further blurring the inside/outside distinction, sometimes, as in the case of the Yuan (Mongol) and Qing (Jin/Manchu) dynasties, taking over as the rulers of a reunified China. From 1931–45, the Japanese tried, but failed, to emulate this trick of foreign rule. Like the Mongols and Manchus, Japan had clear military superiority over China. But unlike them, the Japanese refused to accept or adapt to the superiority of Chinese culture, instead seeking to reverse positions by making themselves the civilized Middle Kingdom and seeing China as backward and barbaric.

Warring States

By far the best-known period of warring states is the one that carries that label (453–221 BC) and that eventually led to the (re)unification of China under the Qin dynasty. As noted, that period is notorious for the ruthlessness and efficiency with which the states within the Chinese system pursued their rivalries with each other. Hui (2005: 156–9) even goes so far as to say that because of the intense focus on self-strengthening, there was no international society within the Chinese states-system at that time. Indeed, this period is often exploited by realists to provide empirical support for their claims about the timelessness and placelessness of their power-political, inevitable conflict view of IR. Yet as Yongjin Zhang (2001: 43–52) notes, during the Warring States period China's practices bore many resemblances to a Westphalian-style international system with an adversarial balance of power and an institution of diplomacy, and with analogies to sovereignty (more implicit that doctrinal) and international law (more in the form of moral ritual than law). But even then, there remained a vestigial central dynasty, the long-lasting Zhou, which kept alive the idea and the symbolism of a unified Chinese polity. Adversarial balancing eventually failed (Hui, 2005), with the Qin victory reunifying the country. The persistence of the idea of a unified China even during periods of deep fragmentation is a key distinctive factor in Chinese practice of international relations.

But subsequent to this defining first period of warring states in China, there were many other, lesser-known such periods. Indeed, it might not be going too far to say that it has been a characteristic of the Chinese system that it alternates between long periods of relative peace, unity, and stability, as under the Han, Tang, Yuan, Ming, and Qing dynasties, and periods of turbulence and conflict when an established dynasty loses the Mandate of Heaven and a multipolar struggle ensues among the successor states and dynasties to replace it. Part of the rationale behind the CCP's claim to stay in power indefinitely is that it hopes to place itself in the company of long-lived dynasties. Sometimes the periods of turbulence are centuries long, as after the fall of the Han dynasty and before the rise of the Tang. Sometimes they are quite short, as between the Ming and the Qing and between the end of the Qing dynasty in 1911 and the victory of the CCP in China's long civil and international war in 1949. In all cases, however, the icon of Chinese political unity established by the Qin and the Han dynasties remains an enduring political framing.

In this sense, the broad pattern of China's practice in international relations fits with the *zhongyong* dialectics discussed above. During periods of disunity and division, the idea of unity and harmony is always present and politically active. Likewise, during periods of unity and harmony, the idea of division and disunity is present and politically active. This understanding is reflected in popular culture. As the famous first sentence of the Ming dynasty novel *Romance of the Three Kingdoms* puts it, 'the basic logic of the world/the general trend under heaven is that it is bound to divide after a long period of unification, and it will unify after a long period of division'.[2]

The Tribute System

Three of the ideational elements discussed above – hierarchy, *Tianxia*, and the Mandate of Heaven – combined to inform and underpin the main practices of the tribute system, with the other two – relationalism and face – playing a more subtle role. While these component concepts were clear in Chinese thinking and practice, the idea of the tribute system itself was not. Zhang Feng argues that the Chinese did not see the tribute system in abstract theoretical terms at the time they practised it. This construction and labelling of it was supplied later by Western observers (Fairbank, 1968; Zhang, F., 2009: 574) and has now become more or less accepted as the way of framing classical China's international relations.

The tribute system started from the Han dynasty (202 BC–AD 220) and ended with the Qing dynasty (AD 1644–1911). It was a hierarchical system with China at the centre, and the scope of application was potentially (but not actually) as wide as *Tianxia*. Under the system, tributary states acknowledged China's superiority thus both recognizing and reinforcing the

---

[2] We are grateful to Wang Jiangli for pointing out this reference and for providing a translation (话讲天下大势，分久必合，合久必分). An alternative translation (from the 2018 English edition, trans. Martin Palmer, Penguin) is 'Empires arise from chaos and empires collapse back into chaos. This we have known since time began.'

emperor's Mandate of Heaven. In return, local rulers received both recognition of their legitimacy and the right to trade with China in the form of tribute. Those sending tribute received from the Chinese emperor gifts of higher value than they presented to him, and the system also allowed a significant degree of private trading alongside the tribute missions. Some rulers in Asia also used the system to their advantage, to gain recognition as the legitimate ruler in domestic succession disputes and occasionally to secure protection from predatory neighbours. For example, the tributary state of Malacca sought Chinese protection against Siam in the fifteenth century AD, and China made a huge effort to protect Korea from Japanese invasions at the end of the sixteenth century (Swope, 2009). During the Ming dynasty there was a neo-Confucian form of foreign policy theory which combined the Mandate of Heaven, reflecting a benevolent and morally superior emperor, with *Tianxia*, as the domain within which the emperor exercised authority. The emperor expected loyal subordination from others and reserved the right to punish them if they disturbed China's peace or good order. This theory extended the hierarchical relations of the Confucian family structure all the way up to the global level and somewhat discounted territoriality as a major political factor (Zhang, F., 2015a: 202–5).

The working of the tribute system, especially its claim to be a relatively benign or non-coercive order, has been subject of controversy. For the most part, it allowed states to submit without being subjugated. China did not undertake large-scale overseas colonization of foreign lands like the Europeans did after the fifteenth century AD. There are of course exceptions to this: the colonization of Vietnam in the first millennium AD and the conquest of kingdoms and peoples to the southwest (Nanzhao, Dali) and Tibet and Xinjiang. Chinese merchants also established substantial Chinese settlements along the trade routes of Southeast Asia, many of which are still there as minority populations. As clearly shown by the famous fifteenth-century voyages of Zheng He, which were about expanding the scale of the tribute system, China used both persuasion and coercion when it suited its purpose. Zheng He's fleets went heavily armed and did not refrain from using force to promote what would now be called regime change in other countries (Chong, 2014: 952-4; Zhang, F., 2015a: 200-2). Geoff Wade (2004: 18-19) goes as far as to liken these voyages to 'gunboat diplomacy', or even 'proto maritime colonialism'.

But the classical tribute system of China was not a coercion-heavy empire in the same sense as either classical Rome or the modern European empires from the fifteenth to the twentieth centuries. As noted above, whether it should be called an 'empire' at all remains a matter of debate (Spruyt, 2020: 156-64). It does not fit comfortably into the categories of Western thinking about hierarchy, though it might possibly be located within Adam Watson's (1992; see also Buzan and Little, 2000: 176-82) spectrum of anarchy-hegemony-suzerainty-domin-ion-empire. It was not even a rigid, suzerainty-like structure but rather a flexible and pragmatic set of mutual relationships perhaps best viewed as a hegemonic form of international society which, more so for its outer than its inner circles, had other institutions such as adversarial balancing and war (Zhang, F., 2009; Zhang and Buzan, 2012). As Yongjin Zhang (2001: 51-5) and Spruyt (2020: 93, 101-10) both observe, the tribute system in practice was flexible and accommodating to the realities of power and the diversities of culture. It embraced many religions and philosophies and was able to absorb ethnic and cultural diversity, as when non-Han dynasties became the rulers of the Middle Kingdom.

China generally allowed those within its orbit to keep their independence so long as they showed suitable deference according to the rituals. While China's relations with Korea epitomized the tributary relationship, its relationship with nearby Japan was much more difficult, with Japan almost never accepting much, if any, subordination (Buzan and Goh, 2020). China's relations with more distant powers such as Russia and the steppe barbarians were in practice (though not in ritual) not far removed from sovereign equality. China was pragmatic enough to allow considerable degrees of variance in the extent to which foreigners observed, or didn't, its cultural norms and practices. China placed the outside world into three circles: those to be assimilated, coercively if necessary; those to be allowed 'loose rein' and political independence; and those to be excluded (Zhang, F., 2015a: 200–2, 210–12; 2015b). Even then, as Yongjin Zhang (2001: 51–5) notes, there was enough pretence at observing the tribute system's rituals to allow a parallel with Stephen Krasner's (1999) 'organized hypocrisy' view of sovereignty. While there was a certain uniformity of ritual across China's foreign relations, with everything having to appear to acknowledge China's central and superior position, the underlying practice ranged widely and could embody relations more like those of sovereign equality. Form was more homogenous than substance.

Yongjin Zhang (2001: 58–63), Barry Buzan and Evelyn Goh (2020), and Spruyt (2020: 133–64) all chart the downfall of the tribute system during China's traumatic encounter with both modernity and the power of the Western states and Japan. Japan's takeover of Korea from the late nineteenth century pulled away China's last tributary. It reduced China from holding the central and superior role of Middle Kingdom to being no more than a sovereign state legally equal to all others, and with the additional humiliation of being a backward developing country well down in the ranks of international power and status.

Conclusions

If we take this discussion of thinking and practice as the baseline for answering our question of 'What would IR look like if it had been invented in China', the answer would have to be along the lines of 'pretty different'. There is some similarity between Legalism and the practices of warring state periods on the one hand, with Realism/power politics on the other. But Legalism and power politics played most strongly in the context of China's internal wars, less so in its relations with non-Chinese cultures. That said, however, one faces the sustained indeterminacy about what the term 'China' encompasses. How does one differentiate inside and outside when the borders between them are in constant flux? Sometimes the northern 'barbarians' were outsiders, and sometimes they were within the Chinese empire, whether as subjects or rulers.

The most striking differences are around hierarchy/sovereign equality and *Tianxia*. As Spruyt (2020: 127–31) emphasizes, the Chinese had a very different concept of inside/outside from that of the West. To risk some oversimplification, it might be said that traditional Chinese thinking about world order privileges the concept of hierarchy but allows some exceptions for equality. This was perhaps not unlike the practice of other 'universal' agrarian empires, such as Rome and Byzantium, and even of pre-modern Europe's aristocratic hierarchies of princes, kings, emperors, and suchlike. By contrast, modern Western thinking about IR theory privileges sovereign equality/international anarchy while making some allowances for hierarchy. When the Chinese faced strong barbarian powers, or remote ones such as Russia, they conceded towards equality. While Europeans from 1648 onwards took sovereign equality as the baseline and the balance of power as a principle against hegemonism, they also recognized privileges for great powers and the reality of differences in power and authority (Simpson, 2004).

Tianxia and the practices of the tribute system represent a radically different conceptualization of territoriality from the quite strict inside/outside view which elevated sovereignty, non-intervention, and territoriality to being core principles of the Western world order. A Chinese IR theory based on it might recognize concentric circles of civilization around a core but not the hard territorial packages that are the foundation of modern Western IR. Indeed, contemporary Chinese practice displays this contradiction, with China being a leading defender of sovereign equality and non-intervention on the one hand, while seeking primacy and a 'return to normality' in its region on the other. This seeming incoherence perhaps makes better sense when viewed through the lens of *zhongyong* dialectics, where opposites are to be managed rather than resolved.

Although *zhongyong* dialectics has not been discussed in relation to the English School, it is noteworthy that both take middle-way positions as their preferred approach to dealing with contradictions. It might well be possible to read international society as a *zhongyong*-style approach to the choice between sovereign equality and international anarchy on the one hand and centralizing imperial order on the other. International society is the middle way, finding a balance between the excesses of national independence and imperial authoritarianism. This might be a fruitful research project for suitably qualified scholars.

Another take on *zhongyong* dialectics points towards an interesting speculation as to whether the rather 'sticks and carrots' style of contemporary Chinese diplomacy, showing both faces at the same time, is a reflection of China's long tradition of having mainly to deal with the militarily threatening, but socially and politically unsophisticated steppe nomad 'barbarians'. Such peoples were, for over two millennia, the main threat to China and the main target of its diplomacy. Most other Eurasian civilizations also faced threats from steppe nomads, but they had sedentary, civilized neighbours to deal with as well. China had no such neighbours and therefore no diplomatic tradition of dealing with cultural and military peers. This behaviour could also, in addition, be a reflection of a rather extreme Sino-centric perspective, in which China defined civilization. From that perspective, all others, not just steppe nomads, were in varying degrees 'barbarian' in relation to it. As S. C. M. Paine (2003: 336) astutely, if somewhat sharply, puts it, 'Only in the late nineteenth century did the Chinese learn that civilization had a plural'.

The Mandate of Heaven also differs from Western thinking, though with some points of contact. It differs from Western dynasticism in giving the people a right to rebel if a dynasty is performing badly. No such right existed under the European divine right of kings. There is perhaps some analogue to the relationship between emperors and subject foreign peoples in the Western tradition and a much more limited one with popular sovereignty's right of the people to choose their government. The enduring importance of the moral order represented by the Mandate of Heaven in China explains the CCP's existential concern about corruption in its ranks and any signs of 'peasant rebellion'. Although the term is not used, the Mandate of Heaven is still a core principle in Chinese politics in the form of performance legitimacy: the idea that the legitimacy of governments derives mainly from whether they do a good job or not. Pines (2012) comes close to arguing that the CCP, despite its self-understanding as a revolutionary party, looks increasingly like a successful rebellion that has founded a new dynasty with an emperor (Xi Jinping), a meritocratic mandarinate (the CCP itself – Braudel, 1994 [1987]: 215–16), and the Mandate of Heaven (the right to supress rebellions and rule eternally, so long as it does a good job of government). So far, this new Mandate of Heaven has confined itself to China, not reaching for *Tianxia*, but it is perhaps beginning to pursue hierarchy in its region and the wider world.

Relationalism sets up an alternative logic of IR that both challenges the Western emphasis on rationalism and is potentially complementary to it. Face is definitely different in importance for Confucian societies than for Western ones, and as a feature of collectivist societies it may also be different in substance. It can perhaps best be understood in the IR context as an additional and important ideational factor in the rational calculation of gains and losses in any transaction, though for those within Confucian cultures it is much deeper than that.

Nationalism was not a feature of traditional Chinese thinking about the rest of the world. The main approach of Confucianism was more centred on cultural than ethnic differentiation, with anyone in principle able to acquire (or lose) 'civilized' status according to their mastery (or not) of the appropriate language, customs, and rituals. But in practice, there was politically significant differentiation between Han and Manchu during the Qing dynasty, with Han nationalism, albeit already then influenced by Western ideas, becoming an important factor in the weakening of the Qing imperium. Although nationalism was not part of Confucian thinking, it might well have become part of an IR theory invented in China once China expanded its range of regular contact beyond its immediate neighbourhood.

5 THE ISLAMIC WORLD

Introduction

Although it is the newest of our three case studies, the Islamic world is in various ways a more complicated story than the other two. It covers a much greater diversity of peoples and cultures than either India or China, and it has a range of polities that differ considerably over time and space. For that reason, we need to unfold its history in a bit more detail. Yet despite this complexity, the Islamic world nevertheless has a significant degree of unity in both thinking about and practising international relations and world order (Aydin, 2018). While that helps to simplify the story, the fact that the thinking and the practice often do not line up well – or at all – makes it more complicated.

Like India, Islamic civilization was in the middle of the Eurasian system. It had direct encounters with others, both civilized (Christian Byzantium, Zoroastrian Persia, Hindu India) and barbarian (Frankish Crusaders, Turks, Mongols). Like China and India, Islamic civilization suffered periodic, and sometimes devastating, nomadic invasions and conquests. At the beginning of the Abbasid caliphate, there was even a direct, if brief, encounter with China (Tang dynasty) at the battle of Talas in AD 751. As noted above, Islam was a 'successor civilization', building on the many legacies of earlier civilizations that had occupied the same territory. It thus incorporated older practices such as reciprocity of treatment and diplomatic immunity (Khadduri, 1966: 53). Islam was also unusual in being initially the religion of a half-barbarian, nomadic people, the Arabs, who had long existed on the fringes of the Mediterranean and Mesopotamian/Persian civilizations (Holland, 2012).[1] The initial Arab conquests brought many non-Arab peoples into the caliphate, and only slowly did these peoples (Berbers, Persians, Turks, etc.) convert to Islam and the Arab language (Braudel, 1994 [1987]: 69–73; Kennedy, 2016: 11–22, 129–32). Islamic polities and empires were different from Christian ones in that right from the beginning they had a fundamental unity of religion and state at their core. While there were many instrumental linkages between state and religion in Christianity, it tended more to separate the spiritual and the temporal and not to define itself as a state. Islam embraced the state form and the close linkage of religion, law, trade, and politics (Risso, 1995: 5–6). Islam was also less attached to core cities such as Rome and Constantinople (Burbank and Cooper, 2010: 71–2). That said, however, Islam was an urban religion despite the paucity of cities in the Arab sphere (Braudel, 1994 [1987]: 50–4, 64–8). The caliphate itself took many different forms. While the caliph was 'the chief executive of the umma' (Kennedy, 2016: ix), that role might vary from something like an emperor to a more transnational role as a spiritual leader. There has been a longstanding debate within Islam about whether the *umma* must have a single ruler or could have several (Khadduri, 1966: 19–22). The principle that there could only be one caliph had broken down by the tenth century (Kennedy, 2016: 284–302), but a kind of compromise lingered on in which a single caliph retained symbolic authority over all of Islam, while its parts were ruled separately (Khadduri, 1966: 19–22). Like Christian empires, 'monotheism was a tool of empire' for Islamic ones, but a tool carrying 'a danger that proved all too real: schism' (Burbank and Cooper, 2010: 61; Kennedy, 2016).

Like India, Islamic civilization was both a major exporter of ideas and a crossroads of the trade routes that linked China and Europe. Since many of the lands controlled by Islam were relatively poor in agricultural production, much of its wealth

---

[1] Khaldun (1969 [1370]: 138–40, 208–13, 263–95) makes considerable play of the relative primitiveness of Arab culture, leading to initial shortcomings in architecture, urban planning, maritime trade and combat, culture, law, etc., when they assumed imperial power.

depended on trade, a vibrant capitalist merchant class, and its fortunate position linking Africa, Asia, and Europe (Braudel, 1994 [1987]: 62–4, 70–1, 75). Commercial culture was strong in Islam (Hodgson, 1993: 97–125). From the outset, it had a keen sense for trade (the Prophet was a trader) and rational economic activity. Islam codified laws for the behaviour of merchants within its jurisprudence and was a 'portable, legalistic faith, attractive to and suitable for merchants (Risso, 1995: 19–20, 71, 104). Indeed, Islamic law (*sharia*) was comprehensive, 'covering all aspects of human conduct' (Piscatori, 1986: 1), albeit there was room for interpretation about how its general guidance should be translated into appropriate behaviour for everyday life. The Islamic world acted as a bridge between the ancient and the modern, and between the East and the West. Islam evolved rapidly from being a desert cult to a highly urban civilization. Muslim traders created a network of trade that linked civilizations from Europe and North Africa to Asia. Islamic innovators came up with the lateen sail for long-distance trading, the astrolabe for navigation, and capitalist institutions, for example, partnerships, contract law, banking, and credit (Hobson, 2004, 48–9).

Long-distance trade was developed and controlled first by Arabs, then Egypt, then the Ottomans. Venice and Genoa profited from global trading controlled by Middle Eastern Muslims and especially the Egyptians (Risso, 1995; Hobson, 2004, 48–9). Andrew Phillips and J. C. Sharman (2015: locs. 1319–416) identify Islam as the common culture of the Indian Ocean trading system before the European intrusion. An Arab writer, Hariri, stated, 'I want to send Persian saffron to China, where I hear that it fetches a high price, and then ship Chinese porcelain to Greece, Greek brocade to India, Indian iron to Aleppo, Aleppo glass to the Yemen and Yemeni striped material to Persia' (cited in Braudel, 1994 [1987]: 71).[2]

---

[2] Khaldun (1969 [1370]: 122, 299–314) acknowledges the necessity, importance, and legitimacy of trade, and the logic of 'buying low and selling high', but holds merchants themselves in low regard, thinking their activities and characters 'unmanly'.

The Islamic world joined hands with other civilizations to extend the foundations of what we today call globalization. Globalization, in the sense of a global trading and financial structure, with all of its social and political consequences, did not begin with the rise of the West after AD 1500. Its foundations can be traced to the Islamic economic networks. John Hobson argues that 'after [AD] 500 Persians, Arabs, Africans, Javanese, Jews, Indians and Chinese created and maintained a global economy down to about [AD] 1800' (Hobson, 2004: 32). Islamic merchants were particularly active in the Indian Ocean, extending both their business and their religion to Southeast Asia and tapping into the China trade (Risso, 1995). While Islamic commerce was not fully 'global' (that had to await European voyages and imperialism), it intensified and extended the Eurasian/African trading economy that had existed since at least 200 BC with the Silk Roads. To be sure, there were other players in this game. Xinru Liu (2010: locs. 790–1153), for example, shows the importance of the Kushan empire in Eurasian trade from the first to the third century AD, which covered the north-western part of the Indian subcontinent plus Afghanistan and much of Central Asia. It was an important link in the Silk Road trading system linking China to South and West Asia and the Mediterranean. It was principally a trading empire, had a syncretic culture (Persian, Indian, Mediterranean, Chinese, steppe), and played a significant role in transmitting Buddhism into China.

The Europeans intruded into the Asian and Indian Ocean system from the late fifteenth century, first extending it to global scale and then hugely intensifying it during the nineteenth century with industrial capitalism. Before that, the Islamic world had created a relatively pacified trading environment with low transit taxes to facilitate trade and a shared, rational merchant-capitalist commercial culture. This was facilitated by the indifference of most of the Asian land empires to sea power and maritime expansion and their consequent willingness to leave such matters mainly to merchants. That said, piracy was a problem in Indian Ocean trade, and one made worse by the arrival of the Europeans (Risso, 1995: 31, 51-2). There were a series of interlinked civilizations and empires: especially Tang China (AD 618-907) and Islamic empires (Ummayad/ Abbasid empire: AD 661-1258; Fatimid in North Africa: AD 909-1171) (Hobson, 2004: 25). The Gupta in India, Srivijaya in Java, and later Song, Ming, and Qing empires in China, Malacca in Southeast Asia and Mughal empires in India also played key roles in maintaining commerce. Another way of looking at this is provided by David Christian (2004: 291, 324-6), who offers a useful distinction between 'hubs' (central linkage nodes in networks of exchange) and 'centres of gravity' (places with a large social and economic mass). Mesopotamia was both a hub and a centre of gravity. The Persians, and later the Mongols, were a hub but not a centre of gravity. China was a centre of gravity but not much of a hub. He argues that the degree of connectivity in these networks was an important source of ideas and innovation, empowering the hubs as a kind of information exchange.

From its position as both hub and centre of gravity, Islamic civilization was able to draw on learning from both past and contemporary civilizations - from the classical Hellenistic world, whose territory it conquered, as well as from India and China; to improve on it by adding its own innovations and insights; and to transmit much of that knowledge to barbaric Europe, especially through the Western caliphate in Spain (Hitti, 1962: 38; Wight, 1977: 34; Wight, 1991: 52; Braudel, 1994 [1987]: 73-84; Hobson, 2004: 175-80; Bala, 2006: 53-62; Lyons, 2010; Belting, 2011; Kennedy, 2016: 153-60). As Nicholas Pelham, the Middle East affairs writer for *The Economist*, notes, 'without the 12th-century rationalist, Ibn Rushd (Averroes), whose defence of Aristotelian philosophy against orthodox theologians influenced people like Thomas Aquinas, the Enlightenment might never have happened' (Pelham, 2016). Aside from Muslim Spain, Italians, and other Europeans also learned some Asian ideas directly through their participation in the Crusades. But once it had acquired Eastern ideas and technologies, the Renaissance 'turned its back on the Orient' (Edwardes, 1971: 94, cited in Hobson, 2004: 174).

Like China and India, Islamic civilization has had many empires, although they were spread more widely and often existed in parallel and in competition with each other. The early Islamic empires, the Umayyad and Abbasid caliphates, approached universalism in respect of believers and constituted a golden age for Islamic wealth, power, learning, and influence (Braudel, 1994 [1987]: 69, 73-84). This age of relative political unity and cultural brilliance was brought to an end by the internal decline of the Abbasids and by the brutal, overlapping barbarian invasions of the Christian Frankish Crusaders (1096-1271) and the Mongols (1241-1312) (Braudel, 1994 [1987]: 85-92). Even though both invasions were eventually driven back, by the twelfth century the Islamic world was deeply fragmented, sometimes with several different empires or centres of power (e.g., the Western caliphate in Cordoba, the Fatimids in Egypt, the Ottoman empire, the Safavid empire, the Mughal empire) and more than one caliph.[3] It was more like India in being often politically fragmented and anarchic, with states that had shallow roots and were often transitory (Katzenstein, 2010: 35). This was because, also like India, Islam provided a cultural and economic framework that was substantially independent from political structures. Caroline Warner (2001: 69-76) notes how in Islamic polities community is the key to rule, not territory, and distinctions between public and private and religious and secular don't operate as they do in the modern Western tradition. Ernest Gellner (1981: 1-40) notes how religion mediated the whole social structure of Islam, not only within and between tribes but between them and cities, in a system that needed to be connected by trade. The Islamic community provided a common framework of law (sharia), language, and commercial practices that both

---

[3] See Hourani (1991: 83-9) for an overview of the main phases of Islamic history.

overcame the ethnic differences among them and differentiated them from non-Muslims (Risso, 1995: 6; Spruyt, 2020:
167–80).

Thus despite its political fragmentation, Islamic civilization
remained a coherent world society with a strong fusion
between religion and society (Bennison, 2009: 47–53). As
Marshall Hodgson (1993: 121, 182, 194) argues, there was
a link in Islam between strong religion and commercial practices and the weakness of political institutions. Political boundaries were 'never fundamental with the *Dar al Islam*'; religion
was the 'chief binding force for the many Muslim peoples' and
there was a strong sense of detachment from transient 'local
military states that came and went'. Arguments about the sep-
arability, or not, of politics from economy and of both from
religion are a longstanding feature of Islamic discourse
(Lawrence, 2010: 171–4). The *sharia* system of law was, in principle and up to a point in practice, universal and autonomous
from secular authority. This intermingling makes the Islamic
view of world order and international relations much less
strongly rooted in political territoriality than most other
traditions.

This political shallowness existed even though, like China
and to a lesser extent India, early Islamic civilization carried
a strong principle of unity in the idea that there should be
a single caliphate. Like India, however, the religious framework
of Islamic civilization, the *umma* (community of believers), gave
it a durable underpinning of social structure that enabled society, and up to a point the economy, to continue functioning at
scale regardless of whether the political structures around it
were strong or weak. Empires and states could come and go in
the Islamic and Indian worlds without too much impact on
society. Empires and states, of course, made a difference by
facilitating more efficient long-distance trade and by providing
security against invaders, and sometimes they could be pretty
durable. The Umayyad caliphate ruled for nearly a century; the
Abbasid caliphate lasted for nearly three centuries (with two
more as a mainly symbolic rump); the Ottomans were a major

force for half a millennium; and the Safavids and the Mughals both lasted for more than two centuries. But many local kingdoms were quite short-lived.

From early on in its history, the *umma* suffered a major ideological/doctrinal/organizational split between Shia and Sunni Islam. In the early centuries of Islam, this schism was not of major political consequence, but it became so from the tenth century with the establishment of the Shia (Ismaili) Fatimid caliphate in Egypt (Kennedy, 2016: 176–86, 235–75). By the sixteenth century, it was embedded into an institutionalized political rivalry between the Ottoman and Safavid empires, adding a degree of ethnic and cultural split (Arab versus Persian) to the doctrinal one, threatening the unity of the *umma* (Khadduri, 1966: 60–5; Hodgson, 1993: 194–5). Ottoman (Sunni) fears of the Safavid's (Shia) ideology precipitated a major military confrontation between them in 1514 in which the Ottomans permanently drove the Safavids out of Anatolia (Dale, 2010: 69–70). Both Sunni and Shia governments often had uneasy relations with the many Sufi sects that populated Islamic civilization. These fragmentations might seem parallel to the various schisms in Christianity, such as the split between Orthodox and Catholic in AD 1054, between Catholic and Protestant in sixteenth-century Europe, and more generally between conservative and liberal interpretations of the faith. The main difference between Islam and Christianity in this respect was that the big splits in Christianity came a very long time after its founding, whereas those in Islam, being intimately tied up with the genealogy and theology of succession immediately after the Prophet's death, came early. Since Islam has both a major role for genealogy from the Prophet's family and a strong streak of backward-looking reverence for its early golden-age years, these splits mattered.

As with our other two cases, we will look at both thinking and practice within the Islamic world as guides to what IR might look like if it had arisen from within that world. An interesting point in this case study is how often these two sources do not line up well with each other, not least because of the political ramifications of the schism between Sunni and Shia variants of Islam.

Thinking

Compared to China and India, there is as yet not much work done on what the Islamic tradition of thought and practice about world order has to offer to IR. The modern discipline of IR is not yet as well developed in the Islamic world as it is in China and India, and it is difficult to find the Islamic equivalents of Sarkar, Tagore, and the many Chinese scholars now bringing China's history and political theory into IR.[4] Indeed, Faiz Sheikh (2016: 4–10, 185–90) argues that the classical texts of Islam offer little or no guidance about international relations because they assume a universal (Islamic) polity, and are based on people rather than territoriality. Islamic ideas about world order spring from the community of religious faith and the conviction that it should be universal, and this is sharply at odds with the Western secular and pluralist foundations of modern IR.

That line of thinking points to another possible reason for this seeming silence: the view that, to a greater extent than is the case with India and China, Islam does not fit well, or possibly at all, with the assumptions about units and practices in mainstream Western IR theory (Turner, 2009; Tadjbakhsh, 2010: 191–2). Shahrbanou Tadjbakhsh (2010: 174) maintains that Islam has 'constructed its own vision of International Relations ... Islam as a worldview, as a cultural, religious and ideational variant, has sought a different foundation of truth

---

[4] This statement may, of course, just reflect our own limitations of language and knowledge. There is an emerging scholarship on this topic in English, such as Sheikh (2016), Adiong, Mauriello, and Abdelkader (2019), and Shahi (2020). In our 2019 book (Acharya and Buzan, 2019: 254), we noted that the modern study of IR had developed quite strongly in Turkey, with several scholars of international renown. It is arguable, though, whether much of this has notably Islamic roots. One exception might be Yurdusev's (2004, 2009) work on Ottoman diplomacy.

and the "good life", which could present alternatives to Western IRT'. Applied to the study of IR, the Islamic worldview has to be treated 'as a paradigm of international theory in its own right'; it is not about 'how states interact with each other or how the system affects the state, but it is rather a concept of world order that focuses on the relations between the Muslim/ Arab and the non-Muslim/Arab sphere and how that realm should be ordered' (Turner, 2009). This rather different theoretical perspective on world order, however, sits alongside a real world in which Islamic polities have, for a long time and especially so since the sixteenth century, conducted interstate relations both with each other and with non-Islamic polities, particularly in Europe (Khadduri, 1966: 60–7). Islam has been comfortable with political pluralism almost from its beginning, and while the *umma* does represent a universal sense of community among Muslims, attempts to mobilize this politically tend to reinforce fragmentation rather than creating a united force (Piscatori, 1986; Piscatori and Saikal, 2019).

In historical perspective, much of Islamic history is also not Arab. While the early Islamic empires could be seen as Arab, this was decreasingly so as the centre of political power moved from Arabia to Syria, Iraq, and Persia. It was Turkic and Mongol leaders that made the Mamluk, Ottoman, Safavid, and Mughal empires. Both the theoretical and historical aspects need to be examined as possible sources for what IR theory would look like if it had been invented in Islamic civilization.

Umma

An important normative idea of Islamic world order is the *umma*, which denotes 'the essential unity and theoretical equality of Muslims from diverse cultural and geographical settings'.[5] Majid Khadduri (1966: 10) defines the *umma* as 'a political community ... endowed with a central authority'.

---

[5] *The Oxford Dictionary of Islam*, www.oxfordislamicstudies.com/article/opr/t125/e2427.

In principle, this religious, people-centred, non-territorial, and aspirationally universal understanding challenges the territorial nation-state idea. But, it does not preclude centralized administration and respect for boundaries and has accommodated itself to territorial fragmentation. The Islamic conception of the state is underpinned by the concepts of *umma* (community of believers) and *assabiya* (community feeling) and may be quite different from the idea of the nation-state and Westphalian sovereignty. As suggested above, in principle and up to a point in practice, the *umma* provides an embracing, transnational conception of community and law that extends well beyond any single state and in some ways, like India's caste system, reduces the functional need for a state. In practice, however, what the *umma* actually embraces is hotly contested. Piscatori and Amin Saikal (2019) argue that there are wide and narrow views within Islam as to who counts as a Muslim, and therefore, matching views on the membership and extent of the *umma*. And, as noted, while the concept works strongly at a level of communal identity, it has an ambivalent relationship with the role and character of appropriate leadership, and most attempts to politicize it have proved fragmenting.

While the Westphalian sovereign state is viewed by some Islamic authorities as a temporary and dispensable legacy of Western colonialism, some Islamic scholars and leaders have also adapted to the principles and institutions of the modern state. Piscatori (1986) makes a historical case that Islam is not in deep contradiction with the state in either its dynastic or national (modern) forms. Fred Lawson (2006: 141; see also Khadduri, 1966: 67) confirms that by the mid-1950s 'the Arab world came to constitute an anarchic states-system characterized by the norm of Westphalian sovereignty'. The idea of an Arab nation, once pursued with vigour by radical leaders like Egypt's Nasser or Libya's Gaddafi, is dead now. Similarly, the idea of an Islamic caliphate that transcends state sovereignty is only pursued by extremist groups like Al-Qaeda or Islamic State, who have no legitimacy in contemporary international legal and diplomatic norms and practice (Kennedy, 2016: 365–75). Most

Muslims and their rulers accept that the nation-state is here to stay, so it is better to work within the system of the nation-state to achieve one's goals than destroy it through Holy War (*Jihad*). At the same time, they, like the peoples and leaders of other non-Western civilizations, rightly consider a singular Western view of modernity as problematic. There are hybrid notions of modernity which can take ideas from the West without imitating it and without weakening the Islamic (or Hindu or Chinese) identity. Japan blazed the trail by modernizing without surrendering its Japaneseness, and China is now pursuing modernity with Chinese characteristics. These hybrids need not pose radical alternatives to Western-derived modernity but can complement it in creating a more pluralistic universalism in world order.

The Realms of *al-Harb*, *al-Islam*, and *al-Ahd* and the Practice of *Jihad*

While the contemporary implications of the classical Indian and Chinese world orders have mainly to do with their current revival as great powers, that is not the case with Islamic civilization. Ian Lustick's (1997) observation remains valid: that it is a distinctive feature of the contemporary Middle East that, despite its long history as a centre of power, since the fall of the Ottoman empire it has been home to no great powers. This situation looks durable. Although Arab nationalism and the idea of a single Arab nation flourished for a while after decolonization, it is now largely out of fashion. Longstanding divisions between Sunnis and Shias, Arabs and Persians remain politically active, now reinforced by divisions between secular and religious leaderships. Despite the existence of great powers in classical Islamic civilization, the relevant debate is therefore more about the revival of traditional Islamic beliefs as a civilizational challenge to Western hegemony and the implications of this for world order.

These traditional framings form around the most well-known and controversial Islamic political concepts relating to the structure of world order: the division of the world into the two realms of *Dar al-Harb* ('territory of war') and *Dar al-Islam* ('territory of Islam'). The former refers to 'territory that does not have a treaty of nonaggression or peace with Muslims', while the latter denotes the 'region of Muslim sovereignty where Islamic law prevails'.[6] From a political perspective, these two concepts seem to make Islam stand much further apart from the Western canon of IR than either the Chinese or the Indian traditions of thought and practice, both of which are recognizably state-based. This distinction is a legal rather than a theological one. On the surface, it suggests a stark realist view of necessary conflict between the two realms, though there is some room for at least temporary peaceful relations between them. There is quite a lot of room within Islam for debate about just how stark, or not, this polarization should be. This problem is complicated by disagreements within Islam about who should count as Muslim, with both narrow and broad interpretations in play. Actors such as Islamic State mark the extreme, with both a very narrow view of who is a proper Muslim and a fierce zero-sum view of how (true) Muslims should relate to non-Muslims (Piscatori and Saikal, 2019; 134–59). This polarization makes no provision for international relations between Islamic states within the *umma* because there is only supposed to be one Islamic state (Tadjbakhsh, 2010: 177–8). The purpose of an Islamic state is to promote, preserve, and spread the Islamic way of life. Unlike in Western thought, the state is not a political end in itself (Tadjbakhsh, 2010: 196). But these concepts were not foundational to Islam and, like the Zhou principles of Mandate of Heaven and *Tianxia*, might have been introduced as legitimizing principles of Islamic rulers as the initial expansion of Islam peaked and competition emerged among various Islamic rulers.

   Dar al-Harb and *Dar al-Islam* are often linked by another, more contested Islamic notion: *Jihad* ('struggle'). Although usually associated in the West with 'holy war', *Jihad* 'primarily refers

---

[6] *The Oxford Dictionary of Islam*, www.oxfordislamicstudies.com/article/opr/t125/ e491.

to the human struggle to promote what is right and to prevent what is wrong'. Khadduri (1966: 15–17) likens it to the European concept of just war. It can be fulfilled in different ways, 'by the heart, the tongue, the hand (physical action short of armed combat), and the sword'. The idea of *Jihad* as holy war was regarded as a misinterpretation of Islamic theology by Arab scholars such as Ibn Rushd (known to the West as Averroes) and is now being challenged by non-traditionalist Islamic intellectuals. Modernist interpretations of *Jihad* stress the Qur'ān's 'restriction of military activity to self-defence in response to external aggression'.[7] Khadduri (1966: 60–70) goes so far as to see the long relationship between Islam and Christianity not just in terms of *Jihad* and Crusade but as a story of the slow development of coexistence.

These concepts in the Islamic worldview are sometimes thought to be so different from contemporary concepts in IR that they cannot be fitted into existing concepts and practices of politics and international relations (Turner, 2009). Yet, this view is misleading. Non-traditionalist interpretations of Islam hold that the distinction between *Dar al-Harb* and *Dar al-Islam* is not absolute and is not applicable to contemporary times. They suggest a third way, which has deep roots in Islamic legal debates, *Dar al-Ahd* (realm of treaties), which holds that peace and coexistence with the non-Muslim world are possible (Khadduri, 1966: 12; Baderin, 2000: 66; Turner, 2009). In any case, the understanding and use of these realms was never clear-cut, and it varied among Islamic centres of power through the ages (Piscatori, 1986; Spruyt, 2020: 220–2).

However, this conceptual framing offers nothing about international relations within *Dar al-Islam* – indeed the very concept is an oxymoron. In this respect, it is interesting to note the work of the great fourteenth-century Islamic historian and proto-social scientist, Ibn Khaldun (Lawrence, 2010: 160–3). His *Muqaddimah: An Introduction to History* (Khaldun, 1969 [1370]) offers a number of insights into Islamic views and

---

[7] 'Jihad', *Encyclopaedia Britannica*, www.britannica.com/topic/jihad.

practices from a perspective between the fall of the early Arab caliphates and the rise of the later Turco-Mongol Islamic empires. Khaldun says little about 'international relations' in the sense of relations among states, other than to note that war is endemic to the human condition (Khaldun, 1969 [1370]: 223–30). He takes surprisingly little interest in the relations between the Islamic and the non-Islamic worlds other than to note the long and very back-and-forth naval rivalry between Islam and Christendom in the Mediterranean that ensued once the Arabs got over their initial unfamiliarity and fear of the sea and learned to stop avoiding it (Khaldun, 1969 [1370]: 208–13).

Instead, Khaldun's political focus is on understanding the dynamics that caused dynasties to rise and fall in predictable cycles *within* the Islamic world. This process he sees in terms of the permanent tensions between primitive, but energetic and strong nomadic pastoralists ('Bedouin') on the one hand and sophisticated, but decadent settled urban civilizations on the other.[8] The Bedouin and the cities are linked by their standing need to trade with each other (Khaldun, 1969 [1370]: 122). But more importantly, Khaldun sees the Bedouin as the main source of new dynasties, bringing energy and strong leadership to counteract the corrupting luxury of urban life. Like Hobbes, Khaldun understands the need for strong rule to control human greed and criminality (Khaldun, 1969 [1370]: 151–2). But he does not explicitly follow that logic, of Leviathan creating a coercive peace domestically, upwards to a logic of interstate power politics and war: 'war made the state and the state made war' (Tilly, 1990; Bartelson, 2018: 49–52). He focuses almost entirely on the internal dynamics, seeing a typical cycle of three generations in which strong Bedouin leadership establishes a dynasty. The first generation is militarily ambitious and capable and expands its rule to the maximum that its skills, geopolitical circumstances, and resources allow. The second generation consolidates rule but becomes decadent. The third

---

[8] Several peoples have played the energizing 'Bedouin' role in Islamic history. Initially the Arabs themselves, then Berbers and Turks.

generation loses its martial virtues, and the dynasty decays and its domains fall away: 'Luxury wears out royal authority and overthrows it' (Khaldun, 1969 [1370]: 115). The degree of central control weakens as the empire expands away from its core (Khaldun, 1969 [1370]: 128–30). Barbarian rule is necessary to renew the vigour of dynasties, but it can also be simply rapacious and ignorant, able to destroy cities and civilizations by undermining law, commerce, and stable leadership. Religion is the way to create 'group feeling' and channel barbarian instincts into more civilized practices (Khaldun, 1969 [1370]: 120–2).[9]

As noted in Chapter 2, Khaldun's perspective could easily stand in for agrarian empires other than Islamic ones. Instead of seeing a world of international relations among a set of relatively fixed units, it sees a general domain that can be either politically unified or fragmented. Its general tendency is to oscillate between these extremes according to the fortunes, resources, and skills of dynastic entrepreneurs. Such empires are conglomerate constructions that can easily both fall apart and be reassembled. This might be seen as a kind of international system but certainly not a Westphalian one. It has neither relatively fixed units nor a clear ideological commitment to either anarchy or hierarchy. It just oscillates between the two as dynastic cycles unfold. From Khaldun's perspective, this form of 'international relations' was clearly the dominant one in the early Islamic world, much more important than rivalries and wars between competing empires, whether within the Dar al-Islam or between it and the Dar al-Harb. One reason that it took two centuries to finally defeat the Crusades was that the then-fragmented Islamic world failed to unite early against them.

Khaldun's indifference to international relations notwithstanding, the general framing of Dar al-Islam and Dar al-Harb does, however, open space for international relations

---

[9] Lawrence (2010: 162) sees the idea of 'group feeling' (Asabiya) as Khaldun's leading sociological concept.

between the Islamic and the non-Islamic worlds. The idea that the non-Islamic world is a realm of war, especially when combined with the strand of universalism within Islam (and all 'universal' religions), suggests a zero-sum struggle far more extreme than Realism. So long as there is a non-Islamic world, the Islamic state should be trying to expand. That perspective is supported by the more radical interpretations of *Jihad*, which take a crusading view of spreading the religion by the sword. Yet Karen Armstrong (2002: 29) argues that, despite the seeming theological obligation to spread Islam, the early Islamic conquests were not motivated primarily, or at all, by the idea of converting the non-Islamic world but more by a desire for wealth and to unify the *umma*. As Hugh Kennedy (2016) notes, conversion of the non-Arabs was a slow process in the early caliphates. So even from the beginning, Islamic practice did not follow doctrine so much as the general logic of agrarian/pastoralist empire.

Just War

Islam also offers, like India and China, a notion of just war. Islam contains numerous ethical prohibitions in combat, as exemplified in the instructions of the first Caliph, Abu Bakr, to soldiers sent to fight the Byzantine empire over the control of Syria:

> *Stop, O people, that I may give you ten rules for your guidance in the battlefield. Do not commit treachery or deviate from the right path. You must not mutilate dead bodies. Neither kill a child, nor a woman, nor an aged man. Bring no harm to the trees, nor burn them with fire, especially those which are fruitful. Slay not any of the enemy's flock, save for your food. You are likely to pass by people who have devoted their lives to monastic services; leave them alone. (cited in Aboul-Enein and Zuhur, 2004: 22)*

Shaybānī's eighth-century legal treatise is very much focused on laws of war (Khadduri, 1966: 4–7).

Epistemology

The modern West credits itself as the inheritor and promoter of the classical Greek tradition of natural philosophy, which refutes divine causation. Yet, Islamic philosophy had a major influence in the development of rationalism in early modern Europe. One aspect of the rationalist Arab theology is the idea of *Ijtihad* (meaning effort) in Islamic law, which implies 'independent reasoning', as opposed to 'imitation'.[10] This method of acquiring knowledge is different from knowledge directly obtained from 'the *Qur'ān*, *Hadith* (traditions concerning the Prophet Mohammad's life and utterances), and *ijmā'* (scholarly consensus)'.[11] This emphasis on 'unaided and individualistic human reason' and the work of Islamic philosophers such as al-Kindi, al-Razi, al-Farabi, Ibn Sina, Ibn Rushd, and al-Zahrawi were a counter to the prevailing 'Catholic belief in the authority of the divine' and stressed 'the centrality of the individual' (Hobson, 2004: 178). Moroccan philosopher Ibn Rushd expounded the 'Doctrine of the Eternity of the World', originally proposed by Aristotle, which held that both time and matter were eternal, not the creation of God at a single point of time and out of nothing. These Arab philosophers did not see any contradiction between religion and philosophy and sought to reconcile divinity with natural causation.

Practice

As we have shown for India and China, thinking and practice do not always line up. For the Islamic world, this disjuncture is more noticeable, partly because the more doctrinal Islamic thinking about world order is less state-centric and more rooted in a religious, legal, and non-territorial social order and partly because the history of the Islamic world is more complicated. Awkwardly for the idea that there should only ever be one Islamic state, which would be broadly coterminous with the

---

[10] 'Ijtihad', www.oxfordislamicstudies.com/article/opr/t125/e990.
[11] 'Ijtihād', www.britannica.com/topic/ijtihad.

umma, the political and strategic reality was often a multiplicity of states and empires and even caliphates. These were both within the *umma* and extended beyond it to Islamic control of extensive lands in which the Muslim rulers were a minority, initially in Syria, Iraq, Persia, and Spain and later most notably in India and the European provinces of the Ottoman empire. Islamic civilization was famously cosmopolitan. One reason for this was its widespread conquests of peoples beyond the initially small Arab world. A second reason was its big role in long-distance trade, discussed above. A third is that it was, in common with nearly all other ancient and classical empires, a slave society, importing slaves from far and wide (Braudel, 1994 [1987]: 58–62; Risso, 1995: 15–16). After the early Arab-led conquests, the military power of Islamic polities came increasingly to depend on importing barbarians, particularly Berbers and Turks, and in the case of the later Ottoman empire also Europeans, as slave soldiers (Braudel, 1994 [1987]: 50–4, 85–92). From the thirteenth century onwards, these imported warriors increasingly became the dominant political class in Islam.

With its emphasis on religion and society, the Islamic world had what would now be called a transnational perspective in both its thinking and practice. In Western thought, transnationalism is something that happens around and through a dominant structure of states. In Islamic practice, transnationalism is much closer to being an *alternative* to a system of states, a kind of cosmopolitanism.[12] This transnational cosmopolitanism is perhaps best illustrated by the fourteenth-century travels of Ibn Battutah. At that time, an Islamic world society stretched from Spain to China, within which an individual could travel more or less safely and have his standing and credentials recognized along the way in both the heartlands and the outposts of the *umma* (Mackintosh-Smith, 2002; Lawrence, 2010: 163–4). This strong transnationalism broadly reflected the historical

---

[12] In Hedley Bull's (1977: 67–8) taxonomy, this would probably place Islam as a 'constitutional normative principle of world politics', a 'cosmopolitan community' alternative to the states system as a basic organizing principle for world politics.

position of Islam as a crossroads civilization at the heart of the Eurasian-African trading system. It was about networks of religion, law, commerce, and ideas that had lives of their own beyond the state.

As suggested above, the concept of the *umma* perhaps bridges these political and social perspectives. If the *umma* is coterminous with *Dar al-Islam*, then it is the self-sustaining social structure that defines how people relate to each other within that realm. As Jane Burbank and Frederick Cooper (2010: 72) note, the *umma* is the space within which 'the boundaries of political and religious communities coincide'. Like the caste system in the Hindu world, it does not preclude centralized administration by states or empires, or respect for boundaries, but it does not depend on them heavily either and it can live comfortably enough with political fragmentation. If, as now, the *umma* is scattered beyond *Dar al-Islam*, with significant numbers of Muslims living within non-Muslim states, then things get more complicated. The idea of a zero-sum game between *Dar al-Islam* and *Dar al-Harb* becomes much more problematic, and room opens up for *Dar al-Ahd*. Amira Bennison (2009: 65-9) argues that the *umma*, despite its many subdivisions, generated a strong sense of transnational community that generally overrode local attempts to customize Islam. The *umma* was Islamic civilization's way of defining inside/outside in relation to the rest of the world. It was also important in providing the framework of legitimacy for political rulers within Islam.

In terms of practice, the more complicated history of the Islamic world benefits, with some risk of oversimplification, from being divided into two periods. The early period runs from the seventh to the thirteenth century and is the mainly (but decreasingly) Arab story of the Umayyad and Abbasid caliphates, when there was a relatively high degree of correspondence between the political (caliphate) and religious (*umma*) domains. The later period runs from the fourteenth to the early twentieth century and is the story of the mainly Turkic successor empires, Ottoman, Safavid, and Mughal, when the *umma* was divided into multiple 'universal' empires. There is a messy transition between these two, with the Turkic Mamluk empire in Egypt (1250–1517) and the Delhi sultanate in India (1206–1526) forming a kind of bridge between the two as political unity gives way to fragmentation. In both of these periods, but particularly the early one, Ibn Khaldun's idea of the expansion and decay of empires, and the interplay of 'Bedouin' and urban civilization, plays at least as big a role as more Westphalian understandings of international relations. Throughout this history, the transnational idea of the *umma* holds firm for most Muslims.

The Early Period

The early period might best be understood through Khaldun's model, which is not surprising because that is the history he was writing about. Under the Umayyad and Abbasid caliphates up to the tenth century, the basic idea was of a politically unified Islamic empire, albeit one in which there was both plenty of internal feuding, often violent, over leadership and succession and a continuous struggle between the centripetal and centrifugal dynamics of empire. From the tenth century, centrifugal forces became dominant, and the caliphate fragmented, with the rump of the Abbasids in Baghdad and independent claimants in Cordoba (Umayyad), Cairo (Fatimid, Mamluk), and Morocco (Almohads). After the last Abbasid caliph was killed by the Mongols in 1258, the *umma* became more or less permanently fragmented politically. All of these caliphates waxed and waned according to Khaldun's formula, and they were mostly too remote from each other to compete or try to re-establish political unity.[13] International relations in the conventional IR sense, other than a more or less permanent war against unbelievers on their two frontiers with Europe (Spain and the Byzantine empire), were not their main concern. What preoccupied them was the internal dynamics and leadership feuds within their empires, which were more domestic

---

[13] For the general history of all this, see Kennedy (2016).

than international politics, though they did involve war, alliance-making, and territory. As Kennedy (2016: 121–4) notes, the early caliphates conducted little foreign policy. The caliphs pursued a ritual war against the Byzantine empire, occasionally negotiating with it for things, such as exchange of hostages (Kennedy, 2016: 107–8). The Abbasids apparently had an alliance with the Tibetans in their brief war against the Chinese Tang dynasty in 751, and the Cordoba Umayyads exchanged embassies with both the German emperor and the Byzantines (Kennedy, 2016: 144–9, 295–302). All leaderships were very much concerned to establish their legitimacy by genealogical linkage to the family of the Prophet. During this period, what might be thought of as the domestic politics of the *Dar al-Islam* dominated over what might be thought of as the international relations of the wars against the Christians in the *Dar al-Harb*.

The Crusades provide an interesting blend of these two. Islam was already politically fragmented by the time of the Christian/ Frankish invasion, and there was both war and diplomacy between the invaders and various local Islamic leaders, with internal Islamic feuds being as important as, and sometimes overriding, resistance to the Christians. Despite the political disarray, the social sense of the *umma* remained strong. This might be thought of as perhaps similar to practice in China, where periods of dynastic unity and stability were separated by periods of political fragmentation, though always with the strong idea of reunification playing in the background of even the deepest fragmentations. The key difference is that China always reunified, whereas once sundered, the Islamic world never recovered political unity.

The Later Period

The later period can also, up to a point, be understood in Khaldun's terms of expanding and decaying empires and the dynamics of interplay between settled agrarian civilizations and nomadic barbarians. But by this time the political fragmentation of the *umma* had become fixed, the expanding power of

European states was increasingly in play, and the model of interstate international relations was becoming increasingly relevant.

As Stephen Dale (2010: 10–47) argues, the Ottoman, Safavid, and Mughal empires all had common roots in the massive Turkic migrations into Iran, Afghanistan, and Anatolia from the tenth to the fifteenth century and the briefer, but highly intense Mongol invasions of the thirteenth and fourteenth centuries.[14] These mass movements of nomadic, pastoralist tribes into areas of settled agrarian civilization caused a long period of political instability and turbulence. The Turkic and Mongol peoples quickly achieved military dominance and, once they had learned (often taught by Persian advisors) that protecting and taxing produced more wealth and power than raiding and wrecking, their leaders became new ruling elites from India through Persia into Anatolia (Dale, 2010: 107–10). But Turkic and Mongol succession customs, like the Arab ones before them, had tribal roots and generated frequent, complex, and fierce succession struggles that often made for weak, unstable, and short-lived states and empires.[15] At the same time, the Turkic and Mongol elites were all influenced by Persian culture and administration techniques, partly acquired *in situ* and partly a result of the scattering of Persian elites by the Mongol invasions. The three later Islamic empires shared Persian-influenced high culture including language, politics, literature, architecture (Lawrence, 2010: 163, 169–71; Neumann and Wigen, 2018: 131–4).

Out of this melange, during the fifteenth and sixteenth centuries, emerged three major durable empires: the Ottoman (forming gradually in Anatolia from the twelfth century but becoming big in the fifteenth), the Safavid (from 1501 centred in Persia), and the Mughal (from 1525, incorporating

---

[14] Most of the Turkic invaders had already been converted to Islam, but the Mongols had not.

[15] As a rule, succession was not by primogeniture but was open to all qualified members of the family/clan (tanistry). This almost guaranteed a struggle for power and favoured strong warlord leaders.

Afghanistan and much of North India). As Dale (2010: 48–53) argues, the Ottomans were a Turkic elite who gathered legitimacy by their military and political effectiveness; the Safavids were again Turkic and gained their legitimacy by the defence and promotion of Shia Islam; and the Mughals were a Turkic-Mongol elite who drew their legitimacy both from military and political effectiveness and from claimed descent from Timur (aka Tamerlane, who built a big, but short-lived empire stretching from Mesopotamia to Afghanistan during the fourteenth century). All three of these empires were susceptible to Khaldun's formula about the quality of leadership. Great emperors generated expansion and cultural 'golden ages', while weak ones invited decay and disaggregation (Dale, 2010). The Mughal and Safavid empires were not major strategic rivals, though they did skirmish regularly over control of border territories and shared Afghanistan as a periphery which they sometimes controlled and fought over, and which sometimes threatened them. But the Ottomans and Safavids were serious and sustained rivals, both over territory (particularly Mesopotamia and the Caucasus) and ideology (the Ottomans being Sunni and not extending their noteworthy tolerance of other religions to Shias).

That said, during the sixteenth and seventeenth centuries these three empires were also connected by a strong trading system on which all depended for both specific goods and tax revenues (Dale, 2010: 106–34). The three Islamic empires all accorded merchants high respect, protected the trade routes from banditry, and provided an extensive network of *caravanserais* along the main routes. Cotton and spices moved from India to the Mediterranean, silk from Iran to the Ottoman empire, and silver from the Ottoman empire through Persia to India. For the relatively poor and sparsely populated Safavid empire this trade was a lifeline, and Shah Abbas I put the Armenian trade diaspora in charge of the trade to the west, while Hindu and Jain merchants from the subcontinent dominated the trade to the east. Europeans connected to this network, putting silver into the system in exchange for silks and spices. It was longstanding practice within Islam to make pragmatic compromises with doctrine in order to facilitate trade and travel between the *Dar al-Islam* and the *Dar al-Harb*. This even stretched to offering safe passage within the *Dar al-Islam* to Harbis (Khadduri, 1966: 10–14, 17–19).

The internal structures of all three Islamic empires discussed here were layered, hierarchical forms of rule that often left considerable wealth, power, and cultural authority at lower levels. Since these empires, and especially the Mughal and Ottoman ones, contained large populations of non-Muslims, this left significant wealth, power, and cultural authority in hands other than Islamic ones. Such tolerance of difference facilitated imperial expansion by making it easy to incorporate new territories. Existing governance machinery could be left largely in place, and no effort wasted having to assimilate the incorporated peoples in any deep way. But when the imperial centre weakened or became less tolerant of the differences, especially religious ones, over which it ruled, it was equally easy for the incorporated polities to break away from imperial authority. Echoing Khaldun's view of dynastic cycles, dealing with internal rebellions, whether resulting from dynastic factions or secessionist leaders (e.g., Ali and the breaking of Egypt from the Ottoman empire) or the rebellions of subject peoples (Sikhs and Marathas against the Mughals, Balkan Christians against the Ottomans), was a regular business of these empires. Like China, these Islamic empires were also fundamentally land-based and, with some exception for the Ottomans, who were at times a serious naval power in the Mediterranean, did little to resist European penetration into, and dominance of, the Indian Ocean (Hodgson, 1993: 197; Paine, 2014: locs. 8482–648).

This fragmentation of the Islamic world into three 'universal' empires, combined with the growing power and reach of Europe, meant that there was a lot more of conventional inter-state relations during this period than during the earlier one. In a nutshell, the practice of international relations for each was as follows.

Ottomans

The Ottoman empire was a highly layered core–periphery structure which often allowed significant degrees of autonomy in its peripheral parts (Bennison, 2009: 53–65; Dale, 2010: 53–62). The organizing principle was to make diversity work for the empire in trade and production. As Burbank and Cooper (2010: 133) put it, the Ottomans allowed 'religiously defined communities' to largely manage their own affairs so long as they 'acknowledged the suzerainty of the sultan, paid their taxes, and kept the peace'. The additional taxes levied on non-believers provided a disincentive for the Ottomans to try to convert their subjects to Islam. They also extended extraterritorial rights to merchants through 'capitulations', which allowed merchants to govern themselves by their own laws (Burbank and Cooper, 2010: 143). Despite this social and economic openness to difference, Dale (2010: 53–62) argues that the principal business of the Ottoman rulers was conquest. To this end, the empire created a highly effective slave army (the Janissaries) that freed it from the military dependence on levies provided by landed aristocracies that typified European states and empires at the time (Burbank and Cooper, 2010: 119). For a few centuries, its military effectiveness and location enabled it to take the role of *ghazis* (warriors on the frontiers of the *Dar al-Islam* acting to defend and extend the *umma*).

The Ottoman empire was a big player in a specifically Islamic international society that also contained the Safavids, the Mughals, the Mamluks, Morocco, and various smaller kingdoms, all of which shared Islamic practices, norms, and laws. The transnational logic of the *umma* played strongly within this Islamic international society: rulers were legitimated in religious terms, and territoriality was much more about frontier zones than hard borders. The Ottomans gained enormous prestige in the Islamic world from their conquest of Constantinople in 1453. This not only fulfilled a major aspiration of the Muslim world, frustrated since the seventh century by the resistance of the Byzantine empire but also gave the Ottomans the most splendid capital city in Islam (Dale, 2010: 77–80). As the Ottoman empire expanded, it absorbed many other Islamic polities, most notably Egypt, which were released when it started to contract during the seventeenth century. The empire warred frequently with the Safavids over territory in Mesopotamia and the Caucasus but also made alliances and truces with other Islamic polities. It was common for Islamic polities to play into each other's dynastic succession struggles.

The Ottoman empire was also part of a wider international system/society with Europe and Africa, with which there was much trade, diplomacy, war, and adversarial balance of power. Both the Muslims and the Europeans saw this mixed system/society with themselves as the core and the other as the periphery. Nuri Yurdusev (2009: 71–9; see also Burbank and Cooper, 2010: 143) develops this line about the interplay/ integration of the European and Ottoman system/societies. He argues that the close interaction between Europe and the Ottoman empire from the fourteenth century generated at least some of the institutions of a coexistence (pluralist) international society between them. The Ottomans played, and were recognized by the Europeans as playing, a substantial role in the adversarial balance of power against Habsburg attempts at hegemony and in great power management more generally. They had an alliance with France as early as 1536, and thereafter a long diplomatic relationship (Dale, 2010: 277). They participated in European diplomacy and may have shaped some of its developments even though they did not accept the idea of sovereign equality and remained distant from European notions of international law. Onuma (2000: 18–22) notes how the Ottomans could not sustain the pretence to sole superiority that the Chinese managed. Because the Ottomans lived in a much more pluralist environment, both within the *Dar al-Islam* and outside it, they had to adapt to getting along with others for purposes of trade and alliance, and this allowed some scope for the development of international law to regulate relations with outsiders. Islam as a religion particularly prized law (Risso,

1995: 5). From the seventeenth century, imperial wars drained the Ottoman treasury without adding new sources of revenue, and the rising European powers began to eat away at Ottoman territory and sovereignty (Dale, 2010: 270-8).

Mughals

Mughal India took over from the decaying Delhi sultanate, which had imposed an often ruthless Turkic/Islamic military imperium on Hindu India for nearly three hundred years (Braudel, 1994 [1987]: 232-3). The Mughals were a gunpowder empire and, like the Delhi sultanate, a foreign minority dominating a much larger local population. They built a rich agrarian empire with a huge army and a highly layered internal structure that provided troop levies and taxes to the centre and a considerable degree of autonomy to the provinces. They had an efficient system of land taxation and a positive trade balance that enabled the import of sufficient specie to support a money economy. The empire had little sense of inside/outside, seeing itself as above all else and potentially without geographical limit (Phillips and Sharman, 2015: locs. 2148-338). It had some border disputes and skirmishes with the Safavids, and both empires not only disputed between themselves over control of Afghanistan but also suffered attacks from it. The Mughal empire was, however, in line with Khaldun's model, mostly occupied with expanding on the subcontinent and dealing with rebellions and separatists. Its authority was shallow, and local governments often had considerable autonomy, which they exploited if they thought the centre was weak (Braudel, 1994 [1987]: 234). The Hindu Marathas attacked it with increasing success from the middle of the seventeenth century. As it weakened, the post-Safavid regime in Iran conducted a major raid on Delhi and Agra in 1739, exposing the decay of Mughal power.

The Mughals were by far the most populous and wealthy of the three Islamic empires but also the only one in which Muslims were a minority (Dale, 2010: 106-7, 126-30). Their attitude towards their Hindu subjects varied considerably from emperor to emperor. Akbar, perhaps the greatest Mughal ruler, was notable, though not typical, for showing great religious tolerance. He conceived a universal religion, called Din-I Ilahi ('Religion of God'), combining Hinduism, Islam, Christianity, Zoroastrianism, and others. The Mughals were not indifferent to sea power but were happy to leave the oceans to merchants, independent coastal trading city-states, or the Europeans. They followed the traditional Indian Ocean trading system based on what K. N. Chaudhuri (1985: 112) calls the 'ancient and honoured law of reciprocity', which meant not 'interfering in the commercial affairs of merchants from abroad' in return for their 'good behaviour' and leaving them to use their own regulations. This meant that the Mughal empire saw no fundamental conflict of interest with either the Portuguese or the Dutch and British chartered companies that increasingly intruded into the Indian Ocean trading system from the sixteenth century. The companies enjoyed a certain military superiority at sea but had to submit to imperial authority in order to trade (Phillips and Sharman, 2015: locs. 1903–61, 2443–514, 3343–92, 3834–4174). In the Indian Ocean trading system, merchants and trading ports both had high levels of autonomy, and foreign merchants were welcomed and protected for the wealth they generated (Chaudhuri, 1985: 13, 16, 36; Darwin, 2020: 4–38). It was the Ottoman empire, much more than the Mughals or the Safavids, that suffered loss of trade as the Europeans imposed themselves on the Indian Ocean trading system from the sixteenth century. Ottoman attempts to challenge the Portuguese control of the high seas were all defeated (Dale, 2010: 123–34, 184–7).

Safavids

The Safavid empire was the smallest and poorest of the three. It arose out of a Shia religious movement and did not consider itself as a re-creation of earlier Persian empires (Parthians, Sassanians) but as something new (Dale, 2010: 69–70). The empire had major conflicts over territory and religion with the Ottomans, and lesser ones with the Mughals over territory. It also had to cope with incursions and invasions from the barbarians to its north. Its most signal accomplishment was to establish Shiism as the dominant faith in Iran (Dale, 2010: 250), though along with territorial disputes this also fuelled the debilitating Safavid rivalry with the stronger Ottoman empire. The major defeat by the Ottomans in 1514 opened a long struggle. The Ottomans feared Safavid Shia proselytizing and so pushed them out of Anatolia, which led to several decades of weakness and political turbulence in the Safavid empire (Dale, 2010: 69–70). The empire lacked sufficient water to sustain major agriculture, and its only assets were the trade and production of silk and its position within the economic system linking the Mughals and the Mediterranean.

Conclusions

Although it has had its share of fairly typical conglomerate pastoralist/agrarian empires, of our three case studies, Islamic civilization has perhaps the greatest divide between its theory and practice of world order/international relations. At least in its theory, Islamic civilization looks quite strikingly different from the Chinese and the Indian cases, both politically and socially. Its theoretical political outlook, defined by *Dar al-Islam* and *Dar al-Harb*, is dominated by a zero-sum religious perspective more extreme than the Realism/Legalism found in any of the others. At the same time, the social side of Islamic civilization had a powerful transnational, world society element that expanded along with the *umma* as Islam made converts, whether peacefully or by coercion, beyond its original Arab base. There are perhaps analogues for this in the sense of community within the Anglosphere or among Indian and Chinese diasporas, but in practice the *umma* seems much more central to the intrinsic transnationalism and universalism of Islamic civilization than any of these other cases of extended 'transnational' community/world society.

That said, however, the practice in much of Islamic civilization bore little resemblance to the theory. There were no clear boundaries between the *Dar al-Harb* and the *Dar al-Islam*, and the latter was mostly not a single Islamic state but an anarchy of competing kingdoms and empires. This 'anarchy' was not, however, of a Westphalian kind. It was significantly mediated by the overarching social unity of the *umma* and by the memory and legitimacy of the early unified caliphates. In this sense, Islamic civilization shared something with China in having a strong sense of a unified whole, but it was not as successful as China in making that into a political reality.

During the period of the three empires, Islamic rule penetrated deeply into territories (the Balkans, Eastern Europe, India) where the majority of the population were not believers in Islam. Furthermore, relations between the three empires, and between them and other Islamic polities, seemed to be far more dominated by dynastic and imperial logics than by religious ones. They were regularly at war with each other over territory, and sometimes also over religious doctrine. They conducted war, diplomacy, alliances, and trade not only with each other but also with Europeans. This was particularly true of the Ottoman empire, which was deeply engaged in both the European balance of power and east–west trade. But the Safavids also made alliances with European powers, and both they and the Mughals dealt with European traders and chartered companies. This record suggests rather strongly that the simple dyadic structure of world order/international relations suggested by Islamic theory had little bearing on the practices of Islamic civilization regarding world order/international relations. The *Dar al-Islam* was itself politically and religiously fragmented, and, at least in the later period, *Dar al-Ahd* seemed to have been much more the practice than *Dar al-Harb*. The *umma* represented a distinctive and significant form of transnational world order that mainly transcended attempts to make it the basis of political mobilization, whether local or universal (Piscatori, 2019). While Islamic theory presents something quite different from Western IR theory, at least some of Islamic practice in the interstate/empire domain, as in Hindu India, seems to align, or be complementary, with Western IR theory and practice.

6 CONCLUSIONS

The main focus of the previous chapters has been on trying to tease out the geopolitical factors, history, and classical thinking and practice about world order/international relations that might have shaped IR had that discipline originated in India, China, or the Islamic world rather than in the West. The purpose of the exercise was to get some traction on what those cultures might bring to Global IR in both thinking and practice, now that they are recovering their wealth, power, and cultural authority. Put starkly, the discussion in the preceding chapters suggests that if Europe's main contribution to the theory and practice of world order/international relations has been about systems of sovereign states and China's has been about hierarchical international societies, then Hindu India and Islamic civilization lie towards the middle of that spectrum. Both have had states, states-systems (international societies), and empires, but both have also had strong world society/transnational traditions that give their world histories and international relations a different profile and balance from either China's or pre-modern Europe's: neither wholly anarchic, nor wholly hierarchic but with elements of both plus significant amounts of transnational cosmopolitanism.

As we set out in Chapter 2, one of the problems with this exercise is that modern IR was largely constructed during the period of extreme Western global dominance in the nineteenth and twentieth centuries. That experience has left a deep and powerful postcolonial resentment within all three of these civilizations, which is a major part of what they now bring to the table as the inputs of the non-West into thinking about, and practising, international relations. Hodgson (1993: 224), for example, nicely captures the humiliation and 'sense of radical spiritual defeat' that the encounter with the power and ideas of the modernizing West inflicted on Islamic civilization and China (less so on India, he thinks, because it was more used to foreign rule). It was a blow to their inner prestige to have their sense of being the dominant world civilization so rudely and abruptly displaced. Postcolonial resentment against the racism, coercion, and cultural contempt of the colonial West and Japan is not going to disappear any time soon and will therefore be a big factor in what the non-West brings to the table of Global IR. Ongoing campaigns against racism and slavery within the West are part of this legacy, and while yet to make a significant impact on the IR discipline's mainstream, they already have a place within IR in postcolonial and other 'critical' theories.

Coming to terms with the legacy of colonialism is necessary to the construction of a viable, deeply pluralist global international society capable of dealing with the rising tide of shared threats. Reconciling this colonial past will not be easy for either side. The West and Japan need to acknowledge their role and accommodate the sense of grievance and humiliation in the former colonial world. But the former colonial world also needs to acknowledge its own responsibilities and complicities: Africans themselves supplied most of the slaves that went to the Islamic world and the Americas; China resisted modernity so successfully during the nineteenth century that it made itself weak and vulnerable to outside powers; the Islamic world likewise proved unable to adapt itself to modernity quickly enough to prevent widespread colonization by the West. The highly uneven onset, development, and spread of modernity initially divided the world into core and periphery. As modernity now becomes more widespread and more culturally differentiated, the huge gaps in wealth, power, and cultural authority opened during the nineteenth century are beginning to close (Buzan and Lawson, 2015). Reconciliation will be a two-way street in which both sides will need to examine their own faults as well as those of the other side. Even the ancestors of today's nice Swedes were responsible for supplying the slave markets of the Byzantine empire and the Islamic world with Slavic merchandise.

But our aim in this book requires that we put this postcolonial element to one side. It is a known factor, if still not given enough weight, in the existing international equation. And as argued earlier, it is not fruitful to speculate about what would have happened if one of these three cultures had replaced the West as the one that first internalized modernity, and then used the resulting wealth, power, and cultural authority to impose a global economy and a global core–periphery structure on the rest. Instead, our main task in this chapter is to focus on the thinking, practices, geopolitics, and history of these cultures in their classical phase, with a view to understanding the kinds of ideas and resources that would have informed the construction of IR had it occurred in these civilizations. As in the West, where Thucydides, Machiavelli, and Hobbes are still on IR reading lists, we assume that the deep knowledge that arises from a society's history, political theory, and traditions of practice would (and will) also play forward into how it understands and thinks about modern international relations. It is this legacy of thinking and practice that modern IR needs to come to terms with if it is to become a truly global discipline.

With that objective in mind, we have sketched out in previous chapters what was distinctive in the world order/international relations thinking and practice of these three civilizations. In Chapter 1 we raised the question of whether culture matters to thinking about IR, or whether materialist explanations dominate to the extent that we might not find significant differences in how IR is thought about and practised across cultures. On the basis of our surveys in the previous chapters, it seems, as we anticipated, that both are true: there is a certain materialist commonality about world order/international relations across cultures, and also some significant difference in thought, political structure, and practice. The times, places, and circumstances of where world order/international relations were thought about and practised do matter, but so do some of the structural similarities of pursuing survival, wealth, and power in a politically fragmented system.

It is intriguing to note that the main schools of thought within modern IR have had no difficulty attracting adherents within the IR communities of India, China, and the Islamic world. It is easy to identify realists, liberals, constructivists, Marxists, and suchlike in all three places and beyond.[1] Now this could, of course, simply reflect the intellectual hegemony of Western IR, its first-mover advantage, and the heavy role it has played worldwide in defining the discipline, setting the agenda, and providing education and training for many of the IR scholars now working outside the West. Yet as Acharya (2004, 2019) argues, ideas from outside do not get absorbed into a local culture unless they can be made compatible with the idea-set that defines and animates that local culture. That process often requires adaptation of the incoming ideas. The fact that the theoretical toolkit of modern IR has been quite readily adopted in diverse places outside the West therefore might reflect not only intellectual hegemony but also a degree of compatibility with local practices and ways of thinking.

This perhaps goes some way to explaining why it is not really possible to make any clear, concept by concept differentiation between those areas in which IR thinking and practice in India, China, and Islamic civilization are obviously either similar, or parallel, to thinking in contemporary Western IR or obviously different. Difference and similarities interweave in complex ways. To sum this up, we return to the six neutral concepts set out at the beginning of this study and use them to review the ways in which thinking and practice in India, China, and Islamic civilization engage with the categories of modern IR in ways both similar and different: hierarchy, power politics, peaceful coexistence, international political economy, territoriality/transnationalism, and modes of thinking.

---

[1] Shambaugh (2013: 26–44), for example, has done a thorough survey of the Chinese IR scene in this regard.

Hierarchy

Perhaps the most obvious difference between our three case studies and contemporary IR theory is that in the former, hierarchy is often the prevailing norm and structure, whereas contemporary thinking and practice about IR are dominated by anarchy/sovereign equality. This difference is easily visible at the level of world order/international relations in the dominance of empires in our three case studies and nation-states in the theory and practice of contemporary international relations. And this difference is not just at the international level but extends deep into domestic politics and society. In our three cases, human inequality was the foundation of human societies, as expressed in dynasticism, slavery, caste systems, and patriarchy. It would be easy on this basis to draw stark distinctions between contemporary IR and the structures and motivations that informed our three case studies. Any such thinking must, however, proceed with extreme caution. All that has just been said about hierarchy in our three cases applied equally to the West until very recently. Slavery was not outlawed until the nineteenth century. Dynasticism was not overridden by popular sovereignty until the First World War. Empires remained the dominant form in the West until 1945. Human rights did not replace human inequality until after the Second World War. And while the rights and status of women have undoubtedly improved from being chattels of their husbands, many structural inequalities and discriminations, and much patriarchal practice, remain. Before the nineteenth century, the West was thus hardly if at all different from the rest of the world in being dominated by stratificatory differentiation in both its domestic and its international politics (see Buzan, forthcoming for the detailed argument on this point). This issue is a main manifestation of the difficulty posed in Chapter 2, that contemporary IR theory is largely a product of the West *since the nineteenth century*, with only a few tendrils threading back into pre-modern European thinking and practice (Buzan and Lawson, 2015; Acharya and Buzan, 2019).

In considering the issue of hierarchy (and by implication anarchy), it is therefore important to keep in mind that we are looking mainly at the period before the West opened up a big power gap with the rest from the early nineteenth century. From that perspective, hierarchy and anarchy mainly mean the degree of autonomy among the units that comprise a particular civilization/empire, and not the situation in the world at large. For example, the Hindu idea of *Chakravartin* does not imply that the Indian ruler conquered or wished to conquer the 'whole world', but the geographic extent of what was then known as *Bharat*. Similarly, the Chinese concept of *Tianxia* was born when the Chinese had no conception of a 'world' beyond their own cultural horizons. Indeed, they were surprised when the introduction of Buddhism and the founding of the Silk Roads, which both happened during the Han dynasty, made them realize the existence of sophisticated, other civilizations such as those of India and of Persia. One implication for IR theory is that anarchy and hierarchy are culturally, historically, and geographically specific concepts. Their application to IR should therefore keep in mind their varied regional contexts, rather than seeing them only from a singular, global perspective.

Waltz (1979) was not wrong in his argument that hierarchy is a fundamentally different principle of social order from anarchy/ sovereign equality. That argument points to a question about whether anarchy or hierarchy is the expected norm of any system of thinking and practice about world order/international relations. Modern Western thinking and practice about IR clearly tilts towards expectations that anarchy, roughly based on sovereign equality, is the preferred and expected norm. At the other end of the spectrum, traditional Chinese thinking and practice – *Tianxia*, the Mandate of Heaven, humane authority – tilts towards expectations that hierarchy based on a legitimate central authority has this position. Islamic civilization seems torn on this question. The theory looks clearly hierarchic, with an expectation of a single Islamic state/caliphate and the construction of *Dar al-Islam* as superior to *Dar al-Harb* and mandated to become universal. The practice, however, is much more mixed and pragmatic. The three Islamic empires all thought of themselves in a general way as 'universal' empires, a common feature in most big CAPEs no matter what their religious base. To that extent, they were hierarchic. The Ottoman empire, for example, did not accept sovereign equality with the Europeans for many centuries, even though it conducted diplomacy with them. But, in practice, these empires functioned pragmatically in an anarchic world, albeit one with little or no pretence at sovereign equality, but rather a rank ordering of different types and weights of polity. India is a more difficult call. Its thinking about world order/international relations mostly suggests anarchy as the expected norm, but with overall hierarchy as both a theoretical option and an occasional practice and rank order within anarchy as a normal condition. This condition of rank ordering within anarchy as the norm, and overall hierarchy as an option, was also the position of pre-modern Europe.

Despite political divisions, there was a consistent Indian (Hindu–Buddhist), Chinese (Confucian–*Tianxia*–Daoist), and Islamic (*umma*) worldview and social order that shaped the political outlook of all states within each civilization. This worldview/order can be usefully juxtaposed against the ideal-type Westphalian model: the idea of a decentralized system of sovereign, secular, legally equal nation-states. Hence, if IR came from Asia and not Europe, it would have been less beholden to Westphalia-like order, even though it might have combined some features of anarchy with hierarchy. Hierarchy would be the norm, whether as centralized empire or ranked anarchy, and anarchy-as-sovereign-equality, the exception. In our three case studies, the experience and legitimacy of civilization-unifying empires would all have been much stronger and more recent than was the case for Europe, which had to look all the way back to Rome, before the peoples and polities of Europe had consolidated, to find any similar inspiration.

Waltz notwithstanding, it may therefore be more useful to think of anarchy and hierarchy not as mutually exclusive categories but rather as part of a continuum, along which all civilizations swing back and forth through history. Adam Watson's (1992) spectrum of anarchy–hegemony–suzerainty–dominion–empire has already been floated in Chapter 4 as a device for looking at different stages of Indian, Chinese, and Islamic history. All civilizations have experienced anarchic periods, the extremes of which were the republican period in India before the Mauryas, the Warring States (itself a suggestive name) period in China, and the post-Abbasid period in the Islamic world. But one should keep in mind that not all parts of what we call China today were 'unified' (a misleading but legitimizing term, which really meant territories brought under control through military force by a dominant power) by its major empires. For example, the Sui dynasty was supposed to have 'unified' China after its break-up (post Han) into the Northern and Southern dynasties, but the territorial extent of the Sui empire was much more limited than China after the Yuan (which added Yunan) or Qing (which added Tibet, Mongolia, and Xinjiang).

China and India have had variable boundaries both as civilizations and as states. But China has had a greater tendency towards political centralization, which is backed by its social ideology (Confucianism) and Legalist geopolitical heritage. That said, however, China's imperial style generally left a lot of local autonomy to its subject states and peoples in return for symbolic and ritual acknowledgement of China as the Middle Kingdom. China's view of world order was certainly hierarchic, but it was not really imperial in the modern, deeply controlling sense of that term. India has been more pluralistic, not only because of its greater multicultural demographic make-up and greater exposure to external civilizational influences but also because of a social ideology which prized tolerance over unification (Tagore, 1918). To a larger extent than China and India, Islam has been a multi-centric civilization with a transcontinental physical scope, with its centres located in Europe, Africa, the Middle East, and Central, South, and Southeast Asia at different stages in history, whereas the cultural and political centres of India and China are always within a more limited geographic area, respectively the subcontinent and the nation-state called China today. This means Islam has been most prone to anarchy and China in some ways least, with India in between.

For IR theory, this begets the question of challenging anarchy and hierarchy not only as constants but also as mutually exclusive categories. What our three case studies bring to the table is a much more open and flexible understanding of the anarchy-hierarchy spectrum. Even Watson's spectrum is too much locked into the Western experience to capture this. What our cases studies suggest, especially the case of the *mahajanapadas* (comprising both republican and monarchical polities) of ancient India and their relationship with the imperial Maurya and other polities, is that IR should adopt a much less rigid, more nuanced and differentiated understanding of the anarchy-hierarchy spectrum. It should recognize a wider range of spaces and consequences in between the two pure types of structure, neither of which ever exists in practice. In yin/yang style, all anarchies (even Westphalian ones) have elements of hierarchy (the special rights and responsibilities of great powers); and all hierarchies have elements of political pluralism. The possible varieties are almost endless. Because Europe was at the opposite end of the spectrum from China in its experience of hierarchical imperial unification, its version of IR naturally featured a rather extreme attachment to anarchy in the Westphalian sense. The early English School founding scholars Adam Watson and Martin Wight both regretted this privileging of anarchy in thinking about IR but could not stop the English School from going down that path (Watson: 2001: 467-8). Both the theoretical and practical realities of IR point towards a *zhongyong* conclusion that the central challenge is to find the right mix within the prevailing circumstances. Our three case studies offer rich resources for thinking about what those balances might be.

Again, Waltz's argument notwithstanding, the real world is often less about an absolute choice between anarchy and hierarchy than about the nature of derogations from either end of that spectrum. As Watson (1992) argues, actual practice over long periods of history points more towards messy mixtures along the spectrum (hegemony, suzerainty, dominion) than towards the pure structural clarity at either end. In other words, both those tilting towards hierarchy and those tilting towards anarchy have in practice always made derogations from the extreme. Clearly in Western practice, but only more quietly in Western IR theory, there are notable derogations from anarchy/sovereign equality in relation to the special rights and responsibilities of great powers, with even hegemony being acceptable if it is consensual (Simpson, 2004; Clark, 2009, 2011; Cui and Buzan, 2016). As noted above, in the early years of modern Western thinking about IR, the 'standard of civilization' was a powerful form of hierarchical thinking about world order/international relations, and this still has strong echoes in differentiations between core and periphery, democratic versus authoritarian, and suchlike (Acharya and Buzan, 2019). In the practice, and again less so in the theory, of civilizations tilting more towards hierarchy, derogations have also been necessary. China in practice had layers of diplomacy that differed between those clearly within its cultural sphere and those degrees of cultural and geographical remove from it. Interestingly, Chen Yudan (2015) notes how traditional thinking about hierarchy is always present in the background despite China's formal (but forced) conversion to sovereign equality. It has to be remembered that China was a big loser from the conversion to sovereign equality, falling from being the Middle Kingdom to being a mere equal with its neighbours and the West. The three Islamic empires all had to deal not only with each other but also the European powers, more or less as equals. They also had to deal with the lower-ranked polities of the Islamic world which had varying degrees of independence/subordination.

On this basis it might be suggested that as Global IR comes to reflect a wider range of cultures and histories, its centre of gravity will probably move away from the Westphalian extreme. The Westphalian bargain around sovereign equality might justifiably come to be seen as parochial: something historically specific to the circumstances of a modernizing Europe/West. Sovereign equality served the needs of a European core that lacked any power big enough to be hegemon; had defeated many attempts at hegemony and come to sanctify the balance of power as a principle; and could increasingly differentiate itself from a periphery that was, especially from the nineteenth century, weak enough to be easily dominated and exploited. That structure no longer reflects the conditions of a post-Western world order, though two aspects of it retain strong appeal. First, sovereign equality is still powerfully tied to independence as the key prize for the periphery of decolonization. Second, the emerging structure of deep pluralism will increasingly display a distribution of wealth, power, and cultural authority in which there are several great powers, many regional ones, and no superpowers, and this points to demand for equality at least among the top powers. Yet against that, some big powers, most obviously Russia and China, are already thinking in quasi-imperial terms about claims to primacy in their regions. The United States is also no stranger to claims either for regional primacy or for special rights for itself, what John Ruggie (2004: 3-4) nicely labels 'American exemptionalism'. There are plenty of historical and theoretical resources to draw on to legitimize such a decentralized world order, and, as discussed in Chapter 4, China is already beginning to do so. The emerging world order will therefore almost certainly represent some mix between sovereign equality/ anarchy and hierarchy/privilege (Buzan and Schouenborg, 2018: 123-61). The most likely forms of hierarchy/privilege will be great power claims to both regional primacy and special rights, such as veto powers, in global governance. But while there is precedent for decentralized world orders, there is none for the combination of that with the high density, high interdependence, and pressing shared fates that mark the contemporary international system/society. History offers no guidance on that, but it does open our minds to a wider range and variety of places along the anarchy-hierarchy spectrum than have been available in the Western way of thinking.

Power politics

Thought and practice about world order/international relations in classical India, China, and Islamic civilization all have analogues with modern IR's strand of power politics/Realism. In India, the realist/power-political thinking and approach was most conspicuous in Kautilya and in the warring states practices of the polities within the subcontinent. There is perhaps no equivalent in India to the Chinese Legalist tradition. Whether this historical strand justifies the current tendency (or obsession) among Indian IR scholars to place a premium on Realism is questionable. Even in Kautilya, power politics was mediated by normative principles, such as attention to domestic legitimation, and based on moral principles rather than outright repression. It may be news to most IR scholars that idealist and normative thinking preceded realist thought in both India and China. In China, the power-political strand comes mainly from Legalist thinking, and from the practice of reconstructing the empire after the failure of a ruling dynasty. The Chinese tradition in both theory and practice is much more pitched towards hierarchy. Shambaugh (2013: 26–34) argues that Realism is the dominant school of thought about IR in China, although one might note that the impact of Marxism (which also peddles a strong line on power politics) continues and that Constructivism (neutral on the question of power politics) has made significant inroads into China.

In the Islamic world, power politics comes out of jihadist perspectives on the relations between the *Dar al-Islam* and the *Dar al-Harb* and out of the practice of imperial and dynastic rivalry within the *Dar al-Islam*. It is strongly present in the thinking of writers such as Ibn Khaldun and Nizam al Mulk. Because, as noted, the modern discipline of IR is not yet all that widely developed within the Islamic world, it is less clear than in the other two cases whether or how this has influenced contemporary thinking about IR. Much contemporary practice in the Islamic world would be easy to read through the lens of power politics.

The power-politics strand provides the main evidence for the primarily materialist view of world order/international relations that discounts cultural factors. It has two essential components: multiplicity and conflict. Multiplicity is identified by Rosenberg (2016) as the essence of the international: differentiated socio-political entities interact with each other in a system/society. In mainstream IR, multiplicity is commonly expressed as international anarchy, a condition in which government is mainly within the individual units, and governance is only weakly, or not at all, present in the system/society as a whole. This generates the inside/outside perspective discussed above in which units, whether kingdoms, empires, or states, or even religious communities, make a strong differentiation between, on the one hand, themselves and their internal socio-political environment and, on the other hand, foreign units and the system/society as a whole, which becomes their operating environment. This structure easily generates both a logic of survival and a logic of expansion, in which other units are seen either, or both, as threats or possible targets for acquiring additional resources. Power politics and conflict therefore easily become a normal and expected feature of world order/international relations. This perspective often rests on a bleak view of human nature as essentially selfish, greedy, and prone to violence. While all three classical cases we have examined display this strand as a prominent line of both thinking and practice, they do so with some noteworthy differences.

In Western IR theory and practice, multiplicity is often thought of as a permanent condition. After it became linked to the powerful differentiator of nationalism during the nineteenth century, it became a lot easier to think of multiplicity as also a desirable condition, embodying the evolved cultural differentiations that are humankind's main social legacy from history. Nationalism then defined the socio-political rationale for inside/outside. There is of course another, more general layer of inside/outside in Western theory and practice. In premodern times this was around Christendom/European civilization as distinct from other religions and civilizations, but under the impact of the big gaps in wealth and power that opened during the nineteenth century this crystalized as the 'standard of civilization' (SofC) (Buzan, 2014b). The SofC differentiated between 'civilized' (i.e., white, Western, modern), 'barbaric' (i.e., yellow and brown agrarian civilizations with urban cultures and sophisticated social stratifications), and 'savage' (i.e., brown and black tribal peoples, pre-modern, mostly small scale, with low levels of social stratification). This differentiation supported blatant forms of hierarchy: the right of those higher up the ladder of 'civilization' and race to dominate and exploit those lower down. The harsh language of the SofC, and the right to use force validated by it, have largely disappeared from diplomacy, but politer forms of more or less the same differentiation are maintained in both theory and practice under terminologies such as 'developed/developing countries', 'core and periphery', 'weak and failed states', democratic versus authoritarian governments, and human rights.

For all three of our cases, multiplicity was not thought of as either a permanent or a necessarily desirable condition, and therefore power politics was as much, or more, about building and maintaining empires as it was about anarchic interstate relations. Their classical writers, such as Kautilya, Ibn Khaldun, and Nizam al Mulk, were all highly focused on the creation and maintenance of 'universal' empires. As noted, both in classical China and in classical India, the notion of a 'world' was confined to their respective civilizational spheres. Before the advent and spread of Buddhism during the Han dynasty, the Chinese probably had no conception of other civilizations like India and Rome (Yan, 2011: 218; Acharya, 2019: 484–5), and their 'world' did not extend much beyond their own immediate neighbourhood. Even thereafter, the Chinese did not see Indians, Romans, and Persians as barbarians or as culturally inferior. With those whom they more surely considered as 'barbarian', such as the tribes to their immediate north and west, Chinese attitudes varied from dynasty to dynasty. As Zhang Feng (2009: 556) notes, the Han, Sui, and Tang dynasties maintained '"brotherly" or equal relations' with nomadic neighbours to the north and west. The Tang dynasty did not insist that Japan, which was setting up its own political system by borrowing heavily from the Chinese political and administrative model in the Nara and Kyoto periods, declare itself as a vassal state (Zhang F., 2009: 556).

It is not unreasonable to assume that ancient Indian rulers saw their counterparts in relatively distant lands as equal. Maurya King Ashoka recognized rulers in the Hellenistic world, including the Ptolemies in Alexandria and the Seleucids in Antioch, as peers. One of his edicts (Dhammika, 1993) refers to them as targets of moral engagement for the spread of *Dharma*, or the doctrine of righteousness. One might think that this was due to Ashoka's lack of military capacity to conquer them, but Ashoka had already renounced war after his decisive conquest of Kalinga in 261 BC (before the edicts were written), and there is no sense here that Ashoka considered them culturally inferior or politically unequal.

Neither China nor ancient India used religion as a basis of hierarchy with outside powers, especially when compared to the Christian West; the idea of Hindutva is a fairly recent construction of the Indian polity, especially of the current, ruling BJP.

In Chinese theory and practice, Legalism allowed for multiplicity and conflict, but there was much less inclination to see this as either permanent or desirable. The idea of the Middle Kingdom carried some sense of inside/outside, but one that aimed to subordinate multiplicity to a hierarchical structure within *Tianxia*. The aim of power politics was not to maintain international anarchy but to restore a layered hierarchical order. This logic, however, was much clearer in the core area around China than it was for more remote actors. At least in practice, Chinese diplomacy could come close to something like sovereign equality when dealing either with powerful steppe empires or with a remote bordering power such as Russia. Warren Cohen argues that the Chinese tribute system before the Yuan and Ming was more attuned to political equality; specifically it was Hongwu, the founder of the Ming dynasty, who 'rejected the international system which had existed before the Mongol empire, a system in which China had diplomatic relations with the various states of East Asia – and other parts of Asia – on a basis of rough equality, sometimes even accepting the fact of Chinese military inferiority' (Cohen, 2000: 151).

In Islamic civilization there was also an element of power politics in both theory and practice, but one that was not necessarily seen as either permanent or desirable. Khaldun's (1969 [1370]: 223–30) view that war is endemic to the human condition covers power politics at all levels and seems to rest on the idea that dynastic cycles are a permanent condition. These cycles of dynastic expansion and contraction within Islam are a form of power politics, but one in which the emphasis is on the expansion and contraction of empires rather than on interstate rivalry. By contrast, the theoretical framing in terms of *Dar al-Harb* versus *Dar al-Islam* suggests a temporary condition of multiplicity between Islamic civilization and the rest of the world that lasts only until all is unified under the *Dar al-Islam*. It makes no allowance for a multiplicity of Islamic states. The practice, however, reflects the pragmatic realities: first, that there often was a multiplicity of Islamic states, as during the three empires; and second, that once its initial expansions had run out of steam, there was no immediate prospect of unifying the world under *Dar al-Islam*. The statecraft of the Islamic empires, both with each other and with non-Islamic powers, thus took on the recognizable power-political concerns of survival and war between a group of polities sharing an international system/society.

What all this suggests is that our three case studies bring to the table of IR a more open view of power politics. They do not see it as a permanent condition or a desirable one but rather one that is sometimes necessary, depending on circumstances. They also suggest a strong link between those circumstances and the anarchy–hierarchy balance discussed in the previous section. This link opens up interesting ground for theorizing. Although the imperatives of 'security against' are still in robust play in world politics, the imperatives of 'security with' are gaining ground as shared threats from pandemics and global warming to terrorism, mass migration, and proliferation of weapons of mass destruction increasingly impinge on global international society. These provide a new and unprecedented set of circumstances in which a less deterministic view of power politics, and a more open view of the interplay of anarchy and hierarchy, might be both useful and necessary.

Peaceful Coexistence

In modern Western IR, peaceful coexistence stands as the counterpoint to power politics. At first glance, it also seems to stand as the counterpoint to empire because empire is about establishing one centre of political control rather than many, and peaceful coexistence requires multiple centres of political power and authority. The logic of peaceful coexistence covers a wide range of strategies, structures, and conditions with which a group of polities can move their relations away from zero-sum power politics. At a minimum, peaceful coexistence represents the pluralist view that there can legitimately be more than one polity in the system/society and that in such a case there are options other than permanent war for those polities to live together. Those options can range from quite limited – some form of diplomatic recognition; agreement on rights, status, and a balance of power; and procedures for negotiation – to quite extensive – development of international law, cultivation of collective projects, recognition of sovereign equality, shared humanity, joint institutions, and such like. Economic relations also fall under the heading of peaceful coexistence, but this is such an important and distinctive aspect of coexistence that we discuss it under its own heading in the following subsection.

In India, Ashoka's *Dharma* is sometimes seen as pure moralism, but in reality it was a pragmatic 'security with' approach, since he left a swathe of neighbouring territories unconquered, even though he would have had the capacity to do so, while retaining in his imperial domain the territories that he had taken by force (such as Kalinga).

Peaceful coexistence is therefore about some form of inter-national/world society. The aims of such a society can be just to impose a few restraints on the resort to war, or they can involve extensive cooperation and the desire to eliminate war. Because Western IR is rooted in the political pluralism of the Westphalian perspective, peaceful coexistence is a well-developed line of think-ing and practice within it. This development, and its spectrum of possibilities, is perhaps most succinctly summed up in the English School's concepts of *pluralism*, representing a minimal logic of coexistence, and *solidarism*, representing logics of cooperation on joint projects such as trade, human rights, and environmental stewardship (Buzan, 2014a: 81–167). Solidarism can even stretch into a degree of voluntary convergence, as within the EU and for proponents of democratic peace theory. Pluralism and solidarism represent different aspirations to both the degree of wanted or expected international order and the degree of difference among the units. The Islamic idea of *Dar al-Ahd*, discussed in Chapter 5, is analogous to the English School's pluralism inasmuch as it seeks merely to curtail, but not eliminate, the resort to war between polities that embody fundamentally different values (in this case religion). The earliest Islamic doctrine was the *umma*, which was exclusionary to non-Islamic peoples but was idealistic within its own self. And if one looks deeply, not only was the Prophet Mohammed called 'the compassionate one' but the Arabs were first and foremost traders, and the early Arab expansion showed a lot of respect for Greek, Indian, and pre-Islamic Persian science and philosophy. There is good deal of evidence to suggest that the early Islamic conquerors respected Jews and Christians as 'people of the book' and that the *Dar al-Harb* and *Dar al-Islam* were latter-day constructs (Armstrong, 2002: 29) that were not foundational to Islam and were rather applied sparingly and flexibly by different political centres of Islam.[2]

---

[2] Armstrong (2002: 30) adds that 'The Quran does not sanctify violence. It develops the notion of a just war of self-defence to protect decent values, but condemns killing and aggression.'

Khaldun's idea of 'group feeling' seems to point towards world society as a necessary substrate for any structure of political order. Khaldun sees 'group feeling' as necessary for the successful construction of empires, and this raises an interesting puzzle. Empires, especially if they understand themselves as universal, are in a strong sense antithetical to peaceful coexistence. Such empires, of which there have been many in pre-modern times, see it as their right, and even their moral obligation, to expand until they incorporate their known world. In one important sense, that principle stands in contradiction to the idea at the heart of peaceful coexistence that more than one polity should exist within a system/society. The Chinese ideas of *Tianxia*, the Mandate of Heaven, and humane authority are perhaps the clearest statements of this perspective. Yet, as we have noted, the practice of such empires is often in fact conglomerate, allowing considerable local autonomy. Even the famously hierarchical Chinese allowed local political autonomy to those polities prepared to acknowledge it as the Middle Kingdom and to concede deference to the emperor.

When this is taken into account, empire can also be understood as being compatible with, or even a system of, peaceful coexistence. It was a common thread in the thinking of 'universal' empires that peace would and could only be achieved once the empire had defeated and absorbed all of its enemies. In this view, universal empire *was the only possible form of peace*. One of the attractions of becoming part of an empire in pre-modern times was to gain a degree of protection, and connection to wider trading systems, in return for sacrificing a degree of local autonomy and status. That bargain could compare well with independent life as a small autonomous power on its own. As Watson (1992: 14–16, 37; see also Buzan and Little, 2000: 176–82) points out, pre-modern empires did not generally have hard outer boundaries but, rather, held degrees of authority over their component parts that tended to diminish with distance from the imperial core. Khaldun also took this view. So long as peaceful coexistence is not defined as requiring sovereign equality among the parties to it, then some forms of empire are compatible with it. In societies for which social hierarchy is the norm, this constitutes a major form of peaceful coexistence.

This imperial way of thinking about peaceful coexistence can blend into a more literal meaning of peaceful coexistence in which polities aim to coexist with their neighbours with limited or no recourse to violence and war. Empires can to some extent be seen in that light, which perhaps goes some way towards explaining how successful they have been. In world historical terms, they are arguably the most durable and successful form of polity, even though they have been out of fashion for the last seventy years. The Chinese system certainly understood itself as bringing peace and order to all under heaven and did so quite successfully, and largely consensually, over long periods. Another, though shorter-lived, example of peaceful coexistence in this sense is the conversion of Ashoka to Buddhism and his cultivation of the idea, discussed in Chapter 3, that international relations should be conducted in a non-threatening manner. This seemed to be more than just bare-bones pluralism seeking to limit war. As we have noted, through his doctrine of *Dharma*, Ashoka wanted to eliminate war, but his initiative is a rare rather than a common example of non-Western peaceful coexistence within a framework of political multiplicity.

While pluralist approaches to peaceful coexistence are generally rooted in the management of state behaviour, solidarist ones more often start from the idea that there is meaning and significance beyond the state in the shared sense of people being part of humankind as a whole, however subdivided by language, culture, and level of development. This cosmopolitan sense (on which more below) is a strong thread of thinking in Western IR, though much less evident in Western practice. One difficulty is that to the extent that cosmopolitan humanism rests on the understanding that all humans are equal, it had little or no foundation in the pre-modern world. Agrarian civilizations generally assumed that all humans were *not* equal. They made sharp distinctions by social rank and birthright, and almost all accepted and practised patriarchy, slavery, and dynasticism as normal. But as Khaldun understood, the absence of a humanist cosmopolitanism did not rule out other forms of 'group feeling', such as religion, that could facilitate larger political orders by providing a wider society to underpin them. Religious communities (Buddhist, Christian, Hindu, Islamic, etc.) provide an interesting halfway house for 'group feeling'. On the one hand, the sense of belonging to that group overrides more parochial differences, but it doesn't reach all the way to humankind as a whole and therefore creates division, parochialism, and often conflict on a larger scale. On the other hand, 'universal' religions open the way to thinking about humankind as a whole in some communitarian way.

The lesson from our three cases is that peaceful coexistence has two sources, which are not mutually exclusive. One is a successful pursuit of power politics, such that one dominant power brings order by ruling all in an acceptably benevolent way. The other is that some shared identity creates sufficient sense of community to overcome the imperatives of 'security against' other people and to enable the imperatives of 'security with' them. Various long-lived empires have been quite good at this game, albeit not on a fully global scale. Classical China is perhaps notable for doing so with a strong cultural element doing a lot of work alongside its material strength. These insights highlight the contemporary dilemma for IR theory. Under the conditions of deep pluralism, anti-hegemony looks like being a strong norm for the foreseeable future. Given the failure of the liberal project to gain global traction, there is a shortage of candidates for global identities to underpin peaceful coexistence. The failure of all of the candidates, both religious and secular, to gain global standing means that they have simply aggravated the degree of global division. Both China and the United States have lost the knack they once had for pursuing this aim. Whether or not the rise of shared-fate threats will open new ground – even if only of the 'we are all in the same boat, and it is taking on water' variety – remains to be seen.

International Political Economy

As noted in the previous section, trade was one of the crucial elements of peaceful coexistence. The need/desire for trade was widespread, both for the goods it provided, both luxury and bulk, and the tax revenues rulers could extract from it. Despite merchants generally being held in low regard socially in agrarian societies, it was a common practice for rulers to make provisions that supported trade and traders. But a formal science of economics/political economy is only a modern invention. The *market* as an abstract idea did not get commonly differentiated from the longstanding practices of the *marketplace* until the nineteenth century (Watson, 2018). But awareness of the advantages of long-distance trade goes back a very long way in human history. One driver of this trade was exotic status goods, such as feathers, shells, silk, and jewels, that could not be produced locally, whose value rose as distance from their point of production increased and which supported the elaboration of social stratification. Another was more basic goods, such as staple foods, building materials (wood, stone), and the precious metals required for coinage (especially silver and copper), that were necessary for the construction of large-scale urban civilizations. There was also, of course, good profit to be made in trading such goods and in providing the networks of trust and credit that were necessary to support the trade. Although classical civilizations, and especially their religions, varied quite widely in their attitudes towards merchants, in practice long-distance trade diasporas were an important institution in nearly all parts of the ancient and classical world (Curtin, 1984).

All of the civilizations we have reviewed participated in long-distance trade and facilitated, or at least permitted, the operation of foreign trade diasporas within their territory. Governments in the ancient and classical world mostly recognized the benefits, and sometimes the necessity, of trade in itself, and they certainly appreciated the tax revenues that could be extracted from the merchants in return for permission to operate and a degree of protection. The more revenue that could be extracted from merchants, the less rulers had to tax their people, though balancing these was tricky. Too much tax on the merchants and they would take their business elsewhere. Too much on the people and they might rebel. That said, trading seems to have been most deeply and positively embedded in Islamic civilization. As noted, Islam was in some ways a merchant religion, and the Safavid empire was particularly dependent on trade as a source of revenue. Despite their ideological and territorial rivalry, all three of the Islamic empires reviewed in Chapter 5 devoted significant resources to cultivating and maintaining the trading systems that linked them both to each other and to India, China, and the Mediterranean.

India, whether under Hindu or Islamic rule, was also involved in long-distance trade from early times. Initially, this trade connected it with the early civilizations of Mesopotamia, and later there were Roman trading posts on India's coast. Already more than two millennia ago, India was centrally placed in the Silk Roads trading networks that linked Eurasia, both by land and by sea, from China to the Mediterranean. India had much to export in terms of textiles, spices, and jewels and needed to import silver in order to support coinage, and also horses for its warriors. Whoever its rulers were, India was generally open to trade, and some of its peoples became well-established trade diasporas along far-flung networks. That said, Hindu civilization did have some stigmas attached to overseas travel across the sea (known as *Kalapani*), but these did not prevent large-scale commercial contacts between Eastern and South India and Southeast Asia, which indeed was the basis of the spread of Indian culture and political ideas and institutions to Southeast Asia (Spruyt, 2020: 253–324).

China was a bit different. It was more remote from the other centres of civilization than they were from each other, and in many ways it was economically quite self-contained. That said, like India, it had plenty to export (silks, tea, porcelain) and likewise needed to import silver and horses. Chinese governments, however, had a fairly erratic attitude towards foreign trade. They linked it politically to the so-called tribute system in which trade was subordinated to processes of political recognition, and understood as an exchange of gifts embedded in a relationship something like suzerain and vassal. While tributary trade was ritualistic and restrictive, with the number of trade missions limited and goods exchanged only through official representatives of the Chinese state, unofficial trade carried out by private Chinese traders flourished, even when official trade had been suspended. China could and did block official trade, both selectively, as against Japan (Buzan and Goh, 2020: ch. 6), and sometimes more generally. When it did so, it suffered from problems of 'piracy' along its coasts. Trade did not so much stop, as toggle from being permitted to being forbidden, meaning that merchants sometimes had to be smugglers or pirates. This grey zone between merchants and pirates was of course also quite common in early modern European practice.

China's official haughty attitude to trade was perhaps summed up by the Emperor Qianlong's famous response to the British trade mission led by George Macartney, late in the eighteenth century, which presented him with the fruits of British industrial technology:

> [S]trange and costly objects do not interest me. If I have commanded that the tribute offerings sent by you, O King, are to be accepted, this was solely in consideration for the spirit which prompted you to dispatch them from afar. ... As your Ambassador can see for himself, we possess all things. (quoted in Kissinger, 2011: 41)

Yet the Chinese did not 'possess all things'. Over many centuries, commercial interactions between Hindu, Chinese, Muslim, and Jewish traders in the Indian Ocean were so regular and extensive that it led to 'freedom of seas' in practice (Alexandrowicz, 1967: 65), even if the theoretical doctrine of *Mare Liberum* was articulated by the Dutch scholar Hugo Grotius.

The Mongols, who were influenced by both Buddhist and Islamic beliefs, famously prized international trade. After building the largest land empire in world history, the Mongols rebuilt and expanded the overland Silk Roads linking East Asia, the Middle East, and Europe into a vast economic network, with roads, bridges, and relay stations, and provided security for traders and travellers. The development of the *Ortoo* system, comprising relay stations about 30 km apart, allowed travellers to rest, feed, and exchange. The bridges built by the Mongols gave merchants free passage. The Mongol contribution to international trade also included the standardization of money and weights. At one end of the system was China, the hub of the Mongol economic and manufacturing system and the world's largest economy. On the other end was Western Europe, which was in the early stages of developing its modern capitalist economy. After conquering China, the Mongols reversed the Confucian principle of giving more importance to farmers than to merchants (Ringmar, 2019: 118). A key element of the Mongol economic network was the system of interlocking economic relationships, known as the *Khubi* system (Ringmar, 2019: 116), among the empire's four segments, the Yuan in the East (Beijing), the Chagatai khanate in the centre, the Ilkhanate in the Southwest (Central Asia and Iran), and the Golden Horde in the northwest on Russia's border. The rise of Europe benefitted in no small way from the Mongol infrastructure and transport network, which became the principal conduit not only for East–West trade but also for the transfer of Chinese innovations such as gunpowder, the compass, paper, and printing to Europe, which was vital to Europe's economic rise.

There can be little doubt that the interest in, and acceptance of, trade in much of the classical world was essentially mercantilist in attitude. Trade was conducted for local advantage, the granting and pursuit of monopoly and other privileges to merchant guilds was normal practice, and there was no liberal understanding or pursuit of the market as a general principle of operation that might benefit all participants. But that was also true in pre-modern Europe, where mercantilist doctrine meant that trade was thought of mainly as a zero-sum game in which the object was to achieve an export surplus and thus draw specie into the country. Europe, or at least the Netherlands and Britain, only fully made the jump from mercantilism to a liberal, positive-sum view of trade and finance during the early–middle nineteenth century. It is impossible to say how other civilizations would have evolved in their thinking and practice of political economy had they been in the lead in industrialization. But it seems clear that Indian and Islamic civilization carry within themselves historically positive attitudes towards trade, not only as a key part of world order but as a sector of activity that should be substantially allowed to organize and run itself, while being supported with public goods (harbours, lighthouses, caravanserais) and up to a point regulated and taxed. There was significant willingness in many cultures to accept that, up to a point, trade should be kept separate from war and politics. The tradition of independent merchants, autonomous trade diasporas, and commercial cities is strong in these cultures. Islamic civilization was perhaps more hospitable to merchants as a class than either Hindu or Christian civilization, both of which did not place merchants high in the social hierarchy, even though they tolerated and exploited merchant activity and developed vast, and broadly peaceful, trading networks. When they arrived on this scene from the fifteenth century onwards, the Europeans initially fused profit with coercion and later resorted to outright imperialism.

The outlier here is China. Confucianism likewise did not rank merchants highly in the social order, but the main line of Chinese practice about trade and finance was much more towards government control than the allowance of independent merchant activity. China often allowed foreign merchants to carry its overseas trade and tried, often successfully, to maintain strict control over them. By constructing trade as part of the tribute system, it entangled it with politics in a way not similar either to pre-modern Western practice or to the practices of Hindu and Islamic civilization. The long shadow of this Chinese tradition is still very visible in its commercial practices today, even forty years after the turn to 'market socialism' inaugurated by Deng Xiaoping.

Our three cases suggest that, as has been the case for the West, long-distance trade is a deeply rooted feature of many civilizations and is autonomous enough to remain in play regardless of whether promoted or restricted by political authorities. During the period of Western dominance in which the discipline of IR grew up, there has been a sustained attempt to create a global market in trade and finance. This has been a very up-and-down affair, with a successful liberal revolt against mercantilism during the nineteenth century; a period of retreat and protectionism bracketed by the two world wars; a partial reopening under Bretton Woods from 1945–71; and a full-blooded neoliberal pursuit of economic globalization, both trade and financial, from the 1980s (Buzan and Falkner, forthcoming). We seem now to be entering into a period of economic nationalism in reaction to the excesses and crises, particularly the financial ones, of this neoliberal period. Our cases suggest that even if deep pluralism takes a contested form, with economic nationalism and nationalism generally powerfully in play, the desire to trade, with its longer historical and cross-civilizational roots, will remain strong. The question will again be one of balance: how to reap the benefits of trade, without having to endure either the instabilities of financial liberalization or the feelings within societies that external economic penetration is disrupting and destabilizing them to an unacceptable extent. Where that balance lies may differ across cultures, and liberalism in its wider sense will be more a source of difference than of common ground. That will be the challenge for a global political economy that seeks to facilitate trade at the same time as both acknowledging cultural differences and varieties of capitalism and somehow containing the excesses of global finance while still enabling it to support trade.

Territoriality/Transnationalism

Territoriality and the idea of a strongly bounded and bordered state are major foundations of Western IR. As a consequence, modern IR theory tends to marginalize empires and largely to forget about their territorial ambiguity and their use of graded frontier zones rather than hard boundaries. This same bias means that modern Western IR theory constructs cross-border activities by non-state actors mainly as 'transnationalism': something that occurs only within the dominant framing of a system/society of tightly bordered territorial states. Mainstream modern IR thus recognizes transnationalism but mainly as an accessory to the states-system, not generally as something possibly independent of, or even alternative to, it.[3]

That perspective is a poor fit with much of world history, both Western and other. Transnationalism is certainly a valid concept in many times and places. It has been common practice for 'non-state actors', whether they be merchants or missionaries or migrants, to undertake activities and weave networks through and around an existing structure of polities, whether kingdoms, states, or empires. Think of the trade diasporas discussed in the previous section; or Christian and Buddhist missionary activists and activities; or the Catholic church; or colonists from many European countries from the sixteenth century onwards. Indeed, transnationalism in this sense of non-state actors forming large and autonomous networks of their own was perhaps a stronger feature of world order in pre-modern times. Pre-modern states and empires generally sought control over their subject peoples for quite limited purposes (taxation and keeping the peace), and while they certainly had a sense of territoriality, it was looser and more flexible than what emerged in Westphalian Europe and consolidated with the modern state there during the nineteenth century.

Yet, the very concept of transnationalism presupposes that political territoriality is the dominant norm in world order/

---

[3] A rare exception here is Bull (1977) 264–81.

international relations, and that is clearly neither necessarily so nor always the case in practice. Think, for example, of post-Roman Europe, where the Catholic church was for significant periods a strong enough institution to rival or even outrank the weak and transitory kingdoms of that time and place. Or think of the Islamic world between the initial Arab empires of the Umayyads and Abbasids and the later three-empires period of Turkic rule. This was the time of the great Islamic travellers such as Ibn Battutah and Ibn Khaldun, whose lives demonstrated the functional reality of a 'transnational' Islamic *umma* stretching from Spain to China that felt more consequential than the ephemeral state structures that came and went within it. Or think of the way in which the great religions spread themselves far and wide. It is true, of course, that Christianity and Islam were partly carried by the sword. But it is also true that Islam, Christianity, Buddhism, and Hinduism often travelled peacefully and autonomously along trade routes, making converts by example and persuasion rather than by the sword. Buddhism was particularly outstanding in this regard, establishing itself widely throughout East Asia, and doing so after Ashoka without any state backing. Chinese culture also sometimes travelled largely by voluntary emulation, and the Chinese concept of *Tianxia* might in part be understood as a way of framing a borderless, non-territorial world in which such movements could happen. Western culture eventually crystallized around the idea of political sovereignty, nationalism, and hard territoriality, but that is not the only possible model for world order/international relations. Islamic and Hindu civilizations were more organized around the principle of strong, autonomous social structures that reproduced themselves regardless of the accompanying political framing: the *umma* and the caste system.[4]

That history provides a different starting point for thinking about world order/international relations than the one that

---

[4] For a defence of the caste system as a social structure enabling many different 'nations' to coexist together see Tagore (1918: 68–93).

informs modern IR theory. At the present juncture, defined by
the shift from a Western-dominated world order to deep pluralism, both territoriality and transnationalism are strengthening.
China is leading the way in reasserting hard territoriality in
reaction against the penetrative excesses of neoliberal globalization. At the same time, the internet is facilitating all manner of
autonomous transnational networks, both civil and uncivil. It is
difficult to anticipate how this mix will unfold. Economic and
environmental crises seem to strengthen both. In a world
increasingly dominated by crises of shared fate ranging from
climate change and disease, through space rocks, to AI 'singular-
ities' and terrorism, the balance and mix between territoriality
and transnationalism may take on greater salience, drawing IR
away from its territorialist underpinnings. If this happens, then
there are plenty of historical resources to draw on from India,
the Islamic world, and Europe, though less so from China, on
how to think about that mix. Bull's famous, but rather
Eurocentric idea of a 'neomediaeval' socio-political structure
built only on European history, but it could be expanded and
relabelled to make it a concept for Global IR.

Modes of Thinking

IR is not just about *what* to think about in relation to world
order but also *how* to think about it. Ontology, epistemology,
and method are all important parts of the debates within the
field. In this dimension as well, there are areas in which cultural legacies play powerfully into how world order, diplomacy,
and international relations are thought about: rationalism
(which is also linked to religion), relationalism, dialectics, and
gender. IR as a field has seen much epistemological debate. One
of these is between 'scientific' versus 'classical' methods, commonly known as IR's second 'great debate', most famously
associated with Hedley Bull (1966) and Morton Kaplan (1966).
Relatedly, IR has also seen controversy over how knowledge is
produced and philosophy of science. Overall, the importance of
rational, secular understanding, explanation, and action, as

opposed to those driven by faith, superstition, or belief in the supernatural, has been a major point of contention in IR.

As noted in Chapter 3, Jackson (2010: 196), while calling for a broadening of IR's epistemology, still holds that for something to qualify as 'scientific', 'it must be intended to produce worldly knowledge'. But what is 'worldly knowledge'? It would seem to exclude knowledge that is derived from religious beliefs systems and the scriptures, where the causes of human or state behaviour, including causes of war and peace, the rise and fall of states and empires, the success or failure of diplomacy and alliances, might be attributed to divine machination.

Indeed, noted IR scholar Robert Keohane (1988: 380) once described the IR community as the 'children of Enlightenment'. But his point that IR scholars commonly aspire to rationality can be challenged, especially when one looks at world politics from a relational prism, as we have discussed in the context of Chinese scholar Qin Yaqing's work. Moreover, as Hobson (2004: 7) shows, European writings of the Enlightenment period tended to view non-Western societies as 'irrational' (as well as exotic, despotic, immature, passive, and feminine), while Western societies were cast as the opposite: rational, civilized, mature, advanced, progressive, dynamic, and masculine. In contrast to the West's 'this-worldliness', including its stress on natural and rational causation and political action based on cost–benefit calculations, non-Western societies were cast as 'otherworldly' or irrational (charismatic and traditionalist in a Weberian sense) with political concepts and institutions that stressed divine or heavenly origins and manipulation of states and rulers. Such a view assumes, implicitly or explicitly, that the West (and the presumed progenitor of Western civilization, the ancient Greeks) led the invention of rational thought, rejecting divine creation, and emphasizing natural evolution and human agency.

But as we have shown, such stereotyping and dichotomous views of the West and the East are false. All civilizations are more eclectic than such a binary allows, containing ideas about both divine and non-divine, rational causation. The emphasis on rational, causal explanations can be found in Buddhism, Hinduism, and Chinese and Islamic philosophy, just as divine causation, superstition, and spiritual claims about world politics are present in Western civilization, including the Græco-Roman civilization, which the West claims as its progenitor (Bernal, 1991; Braudel, 2001, 259). To quote Leonard Cottrell (1957, 179), 'the most perplexing contradiction to modern minds' about Greek civilization 'is between their capacity for rational thought and their adherence to what we regard as grossest superstition'.

As already discussed, some schools of Hindu philosophy, such as *Samkhya*, are staunchly rationalist and reject the divine origins of the universe, accepting instead an evolutionary perspective. Moreover, Indian IR scholarship has begun to explore the place of non-dualistic epistemology, or *Advaita*, which rejects the subject–object, science–metaphysics, inside–outside, rationalist–reflectivist distinctions in Western rationalist epistemology of IR (Shahi and Ascione, 2016). Similarly, we have discussed the revival and extension of the Aristotelian doctrine of the 'eternity of the world' by Islamic philosophers led by Ibn Rushd, before it was transmitted to early modern Europe. The Islamic notion of *Itjihad* also offers a rationalistic and individualistic epistemology, as does the Buddhist worldview in general.

In addition to secular rationalism, there are also some distinctive aspects of epistemology in other civilizations. The case of relationalism and Chinese *zhongyong* dialectics, discussed in Chapter 4, is especially important here. Can it be argued that if IR had been invented in the East, it might have placed more stress on relationality, or at least have been less obsessed with rationality? Although he draws mainly from Chinese philosophy, Qin (2011, 2018) makes the case that since rationalism and relationalism are present in Eastern as well as Western IR and practice, they overlap enough to be combined. Qin's argument is about Eastern societies in general, not just China. He argues that there are profound differences between Western rationalism and Eastern relationalism as approaches to social relations and that these differences significantly affect how diplomacy is conducted and international society managed.[5] Rationalism risks reducing all relationships to mere individualist calculation, devoid of morality, trust, or the dynamics of personal relations. Relationalism is much more about trust and obligation in the process of interpersonal relations within a collectivist social framing. The individual is not understood as a free-standing agent but as a node in a network of relations. It is mainly a person's position and behaviour in those networks that defines them: relationships make people rather than the other way around. Relational logic goes some way to explaining how it is that in Confucian cultures, the actual power holder is not necessarily the person occupying the high office: for example, Deng in China and Tanaka and Ozawa in Japan (Murphy, 2014: 277–313).

One clear implication of *zhongyong* dialectics as a way of thinking is in the perspective it gives on social contradictions. In the Western perspective, contradictions are basically unsustainable. The tensions they create need to be resolved if society is not to fall into disarray. But in the Chinese perspective, as represented clearly in the yin/yang symbol, contradiction is the natural condition of being in society. Contradictions change in form and significance, and need to be handled, but they do not disappear. To the extent that this is true, the Chinese way of thinking is much more comfortable with contradiction than the Western one. One example of this is how people in Confucian cultures so easily combine different religions into their own personal mix, in a way that would seem contradictory to most Westerners (Braudel, 1994 [1987]: 171–2).

This has potentially important implications for foreign policy. It is noteworthy, for example, how the present Chinese government seems quite at home talking about 'harmonious relations' while at the same time bullying its neighbours over

---

[5] For discussion about how Qin's Asian understanding of relationalism relates to the relationalism strand in Western IR, see Qin (2018) and Jackson and Nexon (2019).

territorial claims or diplomatic positions that the Chinese government does not like. It also seems to have no difficulty arguing in parallel on the one hand that a newly risen China should have primacy in its region, while on the other hand being the most vigorous defender of the Westphalian values of sovereign equality and non-intervention. Western analysts frequently see the incoherence of China's foreign policy as a technical problem that needs to be explained and addressed, and they may have a point. Does the problem lie in the decentralized structure of Chinese foreign policy that gives many actors opportunities for voice and action; or in the weakness of the foreign ministry in the party hierarchy; or in the lack of career incentives for party leaders to get involved in foreign as opposed to domestic political issues?[6] But from a Chinese perspective, the pursuit of contradictory policies may not look like a problem at all, just the normal way of responding to complex situations in which policy needs to be continuously manoeuvred between standing contradictions. This idea would be reinforced if Pines (2012) is correct that the CCP is steadily coming to look more like a modern version of traditional Chinese forms of governance. Our case studies thus suggest that foreign policy analysts need to pay less attention to purely rationalist models of explanation and more to the philosophical implications of how such things are thought about in different cultures. In a global international society defined by deep pluralism and a restoration of indigenous cultural authority, such differences will matter more.

On the question of gender perspectives, one has to start from the fact that all of the societies in our three case studies were based on a broad principle of human inequality, as was the West until the twentieth century. Within that, all of the major pre-modern religions and political philosophies treated women as significantly inferior,[7] although there were

---

[6] On the various reasons for the incoherence of China's foreign policy, see Buzan (2010); Wang (2011); Odgaard (2012: 2–4); Shambaugh (2013: 61–71); Garver (2016); Ren (2016).

[7] For a brilliant historical analysis of how patriarchy came to be a universal characteristic of agrarian civilizations, see Lerner (1986).

significant differences between and within religions depending on the ethnic and cultural contexts to which they were diffused and grafted, especially with pre-existing matrilineal societies.[8] So gender as an aspect of thinking about world order is a relatively late arrival into IR, first surfacing during the First World War and interwar years, then being forgotten after 1945, and resurfacing permanently only in the 1980s (Acharya and Buzan, 2019: 94, 141, 239–41). The West therefore until very recently shared the hostility of all pre-modern civilizations to women in politics. Towns (2009, 2010), for example, charts the systematic exclusion of women from politics in Western societies during the nineteenth century. Nizam al Mulk (2002: 176–84) is indicative of the pre-modern attitude. He devotes a whole chapter to the denigration of women in politics, arguing that they have an inferior intellect and should be kept away from power and policy-making. He recommends that should a woman offer advice on these things, the recipient of that advice should do the opposite. It is not possible to say how attitudes to gender might or might not have changed if any of our cases, rather than the West, had become the lead civilization in IR, but there are grounds for concern that the contemporary political re-empowerments of Hinduism, Islam, and Confucianism, not to mention Christianity, remain generally unfriendly to gender equality. To the extent that such thinking becomes re-empowered as the authority of liberalism declines, this issue will become a difficult one for Global IR.

Towards a Global International Relations

We have shown that many key concepts and modes of thinking in IR theory have multiple origins that can be demonstrated from the texts and practices of earlier civilizations. Making these multiple origins explicit should greatly facilitate the

---

[8] For example, Anthony Reid (1988: 629) argues that Southeast Asian societies, despite their cultural borrowings from India and China, retained their 'relatively high female autonomy and economic importance' to a greater extent than was the case with either Hindu India or Confucian China.

development of Global IR by delinking a good part of the discipline's theoretical apparatus from its supposedly Western origins. It opens the path to a more pluralistic universalism in thinking about IR theory. The West may have crystallized these ideas in their current form and given them their current labels, but there is a deeper common heritage of theory and practice that underlines them. We reject any assumption that universal concepts come only or mainly from the West, or that Western ideas are more universal while non-Western ones are 'relativistic'. Keeping in mind that 'West' and 'non-West' are modern terms of convenience, we argue instead that universal concepts can be found in both spheres. Some ideas and institutions that modern IR theory regards as having a mainly European or Western origin are actually found in multiple civilizations. These includes anarchic systems (a system of states without a central authority above them), which existed in Sumer before they did in Greece, India (pre-Mauryan republics), and China ('warring states') and with the Mayas. In many cases, universal orders were pioneered outside what we call the West; for example, the ideas of universal kingship in Sumer and Egypt and the idea of universal empire in Assyria and, most notably, Persia.

The bringing into Global IR of non-Western voices, histories, and political theories will reinforce some lines of thinking and theory within IR, change the balance of other lines, and open up some lines that are now only weakly if at all present. Where there are similarities, it does not matter to this specific analysis whether or not they have arisen from Western IR borrowing some of its ideas from earlier civilizations, though for the building of a more Global IR discipline it does of course matter that origins and credits be correctly given.

Perhaps the most widespread similarity is to be found around ideas of power politics. All civilizations have traditions of thought and practice around this perspective, which makes it a kind of universal in world order/international relations. Hierarchy is similarly widespread, but here there is less close alignment with modern IR. The peculiarities of European history have meant that hierarchy has been subordinated to anarchy/sovereign equality as a theoretical and practical foundation for addressing world order/international relations. All pre-modern civilizations, except Europe, put hierarchy at the centre in thinking about world order/international relations, which means that unlike with power politics there is more of a disjuncture between modern IR and the classical sources from other civilizations. There is a strand of hierarchy/order thinking in Western IR, but it is a relatively marginal one (Watson, 1992, 1997; Lake, 2009; Clark, 2009, 2011). Of particular interest here is the strong linkage between hierarchy and peaceful coexistence in both pre-modern (universal empire) and modern (world government, hegemonic stability theory) thinking about hierarchy. Although a strand of thinking about peaceful coexistence in its own right is also widespread, the strong link to hierarchy has the potential to shift the balance away from the anarchy foundation of modern Western IR and towards more recognition of the understanding that hierarchy is an opportunity as well as a problem, especially if it can be founded on consensus rather than coercion.

There is widespread acceptance in the thinking and practice of Islamic and Hindu civilizations that trade is an important and desirable aspect of world order/international relations that stands somewhat apart from politics. On the face of it, this should reinforce Western IR's rediscovery of international political economy since the 1970s, particularly so given that trade in the ancient and classical world was often framed by deals between merchants and rulers to secure monopoly rights (Ogilvie, 2011: 41–93). The outlier here is China, whose political traditions on trade are much more cautious and restrictive. Chinese civilization had a more political view of trade embodied in its official tributary system, with its unique rituals and regulations, as well as a substantial unregulated or private trade. In China there was neither a wholesale embracing of foreign trade as something that should be encouraged for the general good, nor a willingness to separate trade from politics other than an obligation on traders to pay taxes in return for protection. China politicized trade, sometimes forbade it, and sometimes declined to provide protection, particularly at sea. With only a few exceptions, China's preference was autarchy. When it did trade, China was principally interested in exporting in return for cash, especially in the form of silver, and maintaining a large trade surplus. How these traditions play into contemporary Chinese thinking and practice is an important question.

On the theme of territoriality/transnationalism, as with hierarchy, we find an imbalance. Modern Western IR very much emphasizes territoriality/sovereignty and subordinates transnationalism to that. But there are many strands in the thinking and practice of Islamic, Hindu, and Chinese civilization that offer not just derogations from territoriality/sovereignty but alternatives to it. China's *Tianxia*, Islamic civilization's *umma*, and the peaceful spread of Buddhism and Hinduism from India to East Asia all offer substantial thoughts and practices that question the dominance of the territorial/sovereignty, state-centric approach still dominant in mainstream IR.

In terms of modes of thinking, there are both important similarities and potentially deep differences that will affect the making of Global IR. The main similarity is that all civilizations have a strand of rationalist thinking. Because of the very heavy influence of the United States, with its strong tradition of positivism in the social sciences, on the modern discipline of IR, rationalism is still the dominant strand, and this does provide some common ground. But there are significant challengers to the current mainstream that are likely to come into play as Global IR develops. Qin has identified two of these in the form of relationalism and Chinese dialectics. Relationalism might reinforce existing post-structuralist strands within Western IR. Chinese dialectics seems to open up a radically different ontology about social relations, both international and personal.

At the end of the day, perhaps the big question is how all of this plays into what the English School sets up as the core dynamic of world order/international relations: pluralism and solidarism. Is world order/international relations to be based on respect for difference and collective management of shared-fate problems, or is it to be based on the pursuit of some homogenizing vision, whether religious or secular? All of the civilizations we have looked at here, including the Western one, have encountered this problem and have dealt with it in different ways at different times. The modern West started out with a distinctive, and superior, view of itself. Although it borrowed a lot from abroad (usually failing to acknowledge this) for a long time it had a zero-sum attitude towards Islamic civilization, casting it as the Other to Europe. In the nineteenth century, Europe cultivated a 'standard of civilization' and embarked on a homogenizing mission. Modern Western attitudes have at least partially evolved towards the acknowledgment and, up to a point, tolerance of difference set up by sovereign equality in a pluralist international society. But despite its self-image as tolerant, Western liberalism has promoted a teleology in which all are fated to become like the West. In practice, liberalism has been swift to oppose, often violently, any challengers that threatened either its values (market ideology, human rights) or its teleology of political, economic, and cultural convergence. Whether a declining West will be able to find the tolerance and respect necessary to coexist in a deep pluralist world where power, wealth, and cultural authority are all more diffused is a key question for the future.

Compared to China and Islam, India has been a more internally pluralistic civilization, especially when it comes to its religious and political make up. Being the birthplace of multiple religions, including Hinduism, Buddhism, Jainism, and Sikhism, as well as having had long periods of Muslim rule (e.g., the Delhi sultanate and the Mughals), India is hard to generalize about when it comes to its religious and political pluralism through history. The republics of pre-Mauryan India were part of an 'anarchic' international system which most likely operated on the basis of 'pluralism' in the English School sense. Ashoka's attitude towards unconquered territories, discussed in Chapter 3, and his doctrine of *Dharma* suggest a strong policy of religious and political accommodation which also fits within a pluralistic international order. But even different Muslim rulers of India of the same dynasty have been strikingly different when it comes to tolerance of other cultures: contrast Mughal Emperor Akbar's well-known policy of tolerance of Hindus against his great grandson Aurungzeb's notorious and cruel intolerance towards Hindus and Sikhs. When it comes to Hindu India specifically, it has generally resisted homogenization, but, as with others, this has varied through the ages and under different dynasties. For example, the Hindu nationalism and revivalism of the government of the incumbent Bharatiya Janata Party is at major odds with postcolonial India's explicit embrace of secularism, as demonstrated by Gandhi and Nehru and enshrined in India's constitution.

Islamic civilization has long agonized between the pluralist impulse to tolerate (and tax) difference and the homogenizing one to make converts whether by persuasion or by the sword. It still remains divided in this way. It also remains deeply fragmented both religiously and politically, with these two sometimes reinforcing each other, and with the additional complication of nationalism acting as another line of fragmentation. For the foreseeable future, Islam will lack a great power to represent it at the top table of global international society, instead having a scramble of competing middle powers trying to play that role (e.g., Egypt, Indonesia, Iran, Pakistan, Saudi Arabia, Turkey).

Chinese civilization looks to lean more towards homogenization, but even there the practice was to set up zones where the Chinese would accept difference – but did not want to incorporate alien cultures into themselves – so long as they acknowledged the superiority of the Middle Kingdom and deferred appropriately to the emperor. China is still struggling both to come to terms with modernity (Buzan and Lawson, 2020) and to make sense of, if not reconcile, its simultaneous attachment to both the Westphalian principles of sovereign equality and non-intervention and the traditional idea of itself as the Middle Kingdom exercising primacy over its neighbours.

Traditional Chinese thinking and practices, just like Islamic and Indian ones, do offer resources for dealing with foreign powers outside the zone of the core civilization. But unlike in the extreme case of the anarchic West, those resources are weaker than the ones supporting hierarchical visions of world order and international relations. In the real-world domain of practice, this situation points towards the contested deep pluralism outlined by Acharya and Buzan (2019: ch. 9). The old great powers (United States, Europe, Japan) are in relative decline materially as modernity spreads ever more widely. They are also in decline ideologically, coping with both crises of capitalism and rising domestic disaffection with a liberal ideology that seems to serve the rich much better than the rest. The rising great powers (most obviously China and India) are cultivating exclusionary civilizationalist outlooks (and in-looks). They are trying to combine being accepted as having great-power status and continuing to cling to developing-country status (and therefore rejecting global responsibilities). Thus, although the reasons are different, all the great powers are drifting towards being self-obsessed, neither respecting each other, nor having much interest in taking responsibility for managing global international society.

In the more abstract and normatively open domain of IR theory, the position is more flexible. While a Global IR will have to acknowledge the reality of contested deep pluralism for quite some time, it can also keep open the possibility for embedded deep pluralism and look for pathways towards it (Acharya and Buzan, 2019: 261–84). Under embedded deep pluralism, the great powers would come to at least respect and acknowledge the cultural and political differences among them, and possibly even to value them. The discipline of IR needs to do this too. Just as genetic diversity gives strength, so, it could be argued, does the cultural diversity that is the legacy of human history. The homogenizing visions of the liberal and Marxian teleologies, or indeed any other such visions, would have to be firmly abandoned. The great powers, and global international society more broadly, might also come to acknowledge that they face an increasing intensity of shared-fate problems from climate change and disease transmission, through pollution and threats from space rocks, to issues of migration, cybersecurity, and the management of global trade and finance. Regardless of their views of each other, this situation creates a relentless pressure for a kind of functional cooperation to deal separately with these existential shared fates even in the absence of any generally accepted idea of political (democratic vs. authoritarian) or social (individualist vs. collectivist) values, let alone of global government.

We have shown in this book at least an outline of what the historical thinking and practices of India, China, and the Islamic world are in relation to world order and international relations. We have related these to the thinking and practices of Europe that have been largely responsible for the construction of modern IR in both theory and practice. We hope this exercise has contributed to the parochialization of Europe by showing how much of its thinking and practice was either informed by, or ran parallel to, earlier thinking and practice elsewhere in the world. This exercise exposes the extreme tilt of IR towards anarchy based on European history and thinking and justifies bringing into Global IR the wider range of practice and thinking available from outside the West, which has been forgotten or supressed in the making of modern IR. One conclusion from this book is that, as we anticipated, both material and ideational factors are in play across all of the traditions of thinking about world order/international relations that we have surveyed here. Another is that, despite many differences of style and emphasis, there does indeed seem to be a certain structural quality to world order/international relations that generates a similar range of thinking and practice no matter where it is done. There is a certain isomorphism, but it is not overriding and leaves room for significant (and useful) differences. The choices made in different times and places might well be varied, but the nature and framing of those choices largely makes sense in broad IR terms.

This points to a third, more pragmatic, conclusion, which is that the making of Global IR might not be so difficult as could be imagined. It is not, as might be feared, a question of how to pull together a highly diverse and incompatible set of histories and theories. A great deal of what we have surveyed in terms of thinking and practice displays common ground. There are certainly substantial differences of emphasis and focus, and some ideas and concepts that are outside the existing lexicon. But many of these differences can be incorporated within existing lines of thought and theory within IR, expanding, enriching, and complementing them, and also challenging them in various ways. Much that went into 'Western IR' came from outside the West, and it seems clear from our analysis that it would be easier for Western IR to see this if it took on board not just the history and thinking of other civilizations but also more of Western history before the nineteenth century, when in many ways the West was less different from the rest of the world (i.e., likewise being a patriarchal, dynastic, slave-owning, religious culture with a more open sense of territoriality).

Global IR, as we have argued before (Acharya and Buzan, 2019), does not and cannot displace existing IR theories. At the same time, it does not leave them as is but challenges them to ground themselves in world history and to incorporate the voices, experiences, and contributions of non-Western civilizations and states.

Some scholars based in the West see work on IR and area studies drawing on non-Western histories as 'culturalism' or 'civilizationalism' and insist that such work must be integrated into a discourse on 'global modernity' (Dalacoura, 2020). Yet the very notion of a 'global modernity' has a deeply problematic basis in Western imperialism and dominance. Our position is that the ideas and institutions of non-Western societies deserve to be studied on their own terms. To be sure, comparative work involving different societies and their relationship with a still West-dominated IR theory are welcome; indeed, this is exactly what we do in this book. But such work should not be expected to fit within some arbitrary notion of 'modernity'. Global modernity should not become a pretext for reaffirming a singular, Western-dominated idea of 'modernity' while rejecting or marginalizing the ideas and voices of societies and scholars from the non-Western world. As far as Global IR is concerned, there is no such Europe-derived 'global modernity' but what S. N. Eisenstadt (2000) among others has called 'multiple modernities'. All cultures are transformed by the encounter with modernity, just as Europe's was, but as Rosenberg's (2010, 2013, 2016) theory of uneven and combined development makes clear, all find their own distinctive way of dealing with that encounter.

In reality, the goal of Global IR from the very outset has been precisely the opposite: to reject 'cultural exceptionalism and parochialism', including 'the tendency to present the characteristics of one's own group (society, state, or civilization) as homogenous, unique, and superior to those of others' (Acharya, 2014: 615). As Acharya (2014: 651) had recognized and warned against in explicating the idea of Global IR:

> a truly Global IR must eschew cultural exceptionalism and parochialism .... Claims about exceptionalism frequently fall apart not just because of the cultural and political diversity within nations, regions, and civilizations. Such claims reflect the political agendas and purposes of the ruling elite, as evident in concepts such as 'Asian Values,' 'Asian human rights,' or 'Asian Democracy' – which critics rightly associated with authoritarianism. Similarly, exceptionalism often justifies the dominance of the powerful states over the weak. American exceptionalism, seemingly benign and popular at home, finds expression in the Monroe Doctrine and its self-serving global interventionism. One strand of Japan's prewar pan-Asian discourse – founded upon the slogan of 'Asia for Asians' – also illustrates this tendency. Some efforts to invoke the Chinese tributary system as the basis of a new Chinese School of IR raise similar possibilities.'

The temptation to flaunt and use civilizational achievements for domestic consumption and a foreign policy approach exists in both the West and the Rest, who label and attack non-Western voices in IR as 'nativistic' or 'ethnicist' (Alejandro, 2018: 182),[9] while Western scholarship – whether mainstream or critical theory is regarded as universal – could turn out to be another way of silencing non-Western scholars from engaging with IR theory and another weapon against scholars who study their own cultures and civilizations to challenge IR's profound and persistent Eurocentrism.

Indeed, the study of non-Western histories and cultures is crucial to decolonizing IR, which has been a key goal of Global IR from its inception. As Eleanor Newbigin (2019) argues, decolonizing history (or IR or any branch of social sciences and humanities) means exploring why and how ideas that inform and dominate these disciplines 'emerged and continue to shape our understanding of not only the world under European empire but *also before that.* Indeed, a fundamental part of undoing the blinkers of colonised history is to teach more widely and actively about *attitudes and world views that existed before European empire,* while thinking about why and how these came to be side-lined later on.' (emphasis added).

We are also acutely aware of the risk that scholars in the non-Western world who seek to engage with IR theory by drawing on historical concepts and practices from their own cultures, be it India, China, or Islam, can sometimes end up justifying the actions – good or bad – of their own governments. But this is not always the case and the danger is not insurmountable.[10]One

---

[9] 'Native' in India goes as a colonial-era epithet for Indians, associated with laziness and inferior capabilities. Alejandro also considers Acharya's call for using Franz Fanon's work to build non-Western IR theory as an example of 'ethnicism' (Alejandro, 2018: 182)

[10] To avoid cultural exceptionalism, Acharya (2019: 494) has written, in the context of the 'Chinese School of IR', that national and regional approaches

1. should be able to travel beyond the country of their origin (in this case China) and its immediate neighbourhood (East Asia) and offer a more general framework for analyzing world affairs;
2. should attract a critical mass of scholars within and beyond the country of their origin;
3. should generate a vibrant research agenda, meaning they should be taken up and applied by other scholars, especially students and new

should always keep in mind Robert Cox's (1986: 207) famous line: 'Theory is always *for* someone and *for* some purpose', but this applies as much to scholars from the West as to those from the Rest, as much to mainstream theories such as Realism, Liberalism, and Constructivism as to critical theories such as Postmodernism, Postcolonialism, and Reflexivist approaches.

But there are numerous scholars in the Global South who are genuinely interested in the historical ideas and approaches of their own nations for mainly academic purposes.[11] In many cases, the aim is not to glorify their governments but to look to their own histories to derive concepts and approaches that would enable them to engage in IR theory with their counterparts in the West. The Global IR project seeks to embrace such voices, to find intellectual space for the ideas and experiences from both worlds, and to stimulate a conversation across cultures and societies. At the same time, the academic–policy nexus is not unique to the non-Western world. In the West, academics from Alfred Zimmern, through Henry Kissinger, to Anne Marie Slaughter, to name but a very few, have engaged in policy work, sometimes supporting and legitimizing the policy of their governments and their 'civilizations' without being accused of being 'civilizationist' or 'nativist'.

Against this backdrop, we believe that while a truly Global IR might retain some of the broad categories and arguments of the present IR, it would also, by introducing ideas and practices from other societies, including India, China, and Islam, transform IR to a discipline with richer and more varied theoretical foundations and more wide-ranging and diverse strands of empirical examples. Global IR will also need to distance itself

---

generations of scholars, to develop their own research and theoretical contribution;

4.   should enjoy some longevity and not turn out to be a passing fad;

5.   should maintain some distance from official policy of the country of their origin.

[11] In India, for example, several established and emerging scholars – Navnita Behera (2007), Siddharth Mallavarapu (2009), and Deepshikha Shahi (2014, 2018, 2020b) – have written on non-Western IR theory, and Global IR, from a purely academic interest, without official connections with the Indian government or supporting its foreign policy.

from the mainly Western view of world history on which it currently rests. It needs to do more than just adding other histories to a Western one that remains at the core. Global IR needs to be backed by a properly global history that takes humankind as its central reference and places the various civilizations within that overarching framing.

With a richer and more diverse foundation, IR will look and act different. It might take on a more relational, hierarchical, and possibly historical/civilizational make-up, covering both epistemology and ontology. Territoriality and transnationalism, for example, would fall into a much longer and deeper historical perspective, as would the semi-independent role of trade. Peaceful coexistence would have to incorporate more hierarchical approaches, and economic nationalism would have equal place with the liberal teleology in international political economy. Modes of thinking would have to incorporate a wider range of ontologies and epistemologies. The balance among the strands might also change, with hierarchy taking equal place with anarchy, and power politics and peaceful coexistence being seen more as a linked pair, like order and justice, than as alternate routes. Given the commonalities, it might be easier for everyone to share the house of IR than one might have thought initially. It would require more openness and willingness to coexist than is apparent at present, but the much lamented 'fragmentation' of IR might prove a strength rather than a weakness in undertaking this rebuilding and refurbishment. The subject is so big and deep that it benefits from the many lenses that different approaches can bring to it. These theoretical lenses, like the physical ones used in the natural sciences, each bring some things into clearer focus while obscuring others. Fragmentation is certainly a problem for those looking for a single unified theory of IR. For the rest of us, the game is one of 'pluralistic universalism' (Acharya, 2014): trying to link, and understand the interactions among, all of these partial views.

Perhaps the biggest obstacle to achieving Global IR is getting around the way that the existing construct of IR is stamped as a Western brand. There are elements of the old tensions over the 'standard of civilization' in this situation, with some being pushed to defend it and others to attack it. Some, perhaps many, will feel awkward about integrating in this way, preferring oppositionalism to engagement. Certainly, Global IR will have to confront the difficult questions raised by IR's links to colonialism and racism. Those questions will always cause controversy, and that controversy needs to be a more central issue for Global IR than it is so far. A lot of what has been forgotten by both sides needs to be put on the table and discussed. Indeed, it might be argued that confronting the colonial and postcolonial questions and arguing them out is the necessary rite of passage for making Global IR.

REFERENCES

Aboul-Enein, H. Yousuf, and Sherifa Zuhur (2004) *Islamic Rulings on Warfare*, Darby, PA: Diane Publishing Co.

Acharya, Amitav (2003-4) 'Will Asia's Past Be Its Future?', *International Security*, 28:3, 149-64.

Acharya, Amitav (2004) 'How Ideas Spread, Whose Norms Matter: Norm Localization and Institutional Change in Asian Regionalism', *International Organization*, 58:2, 239-75.

Acharya, Amitav (2011) 'Dialogue and Discovery: In Search of International Relations Theories beyond the West', *Millennium: Journal of International Studies*, 39:3, 619-37.

Acharya, Amitav (2012) *Civilizations in Embrace: The Spread of Ideas and the Transformation of Power*, Singapore: Institute of Southeast Asian Studies.

Acharya, Amitav (2014) 'Global International Relations (IR) and Regional Worlds: A New Agenda for International Studies', *International Studies Quarterly*, 58:4, 647-59.

Acharya, Amitav (2019) 'From Heaven to Earth: "Cultural Idealism" and "Moral Realism" As Chinese Contributions to Global International Relations', *Chinese Journal of International Politics*, 12:4, 467-94.

Acharya, Amitav, and Barry Buzan (2007) 'Conclusion: On the Possibility of a Non-Western IR Theory in Asia', *International Relations of the Asia-Pacific*, 7:3, 427-38.

Acharya, Amitav, and Barry Buzan (2019) *The Making of Global International Relations: Origins and Evolution of IR at Its Centenary*, Cambridge: Cambridge University Press.

Adiong, Nassef M., Raffaele Mauriello, and Deina Abdelkader (eds) (2019) *Islam in International Relations: Politics and Paradigms*, London: Routledge.

Alejandro, Audrey (2018) *Western Dominance in International Relations: The Internationalization of IR in Brazil and India*, London: Routledge.

Alexandrowicz, Charles H. (1967) *An Introduction to the History of the Law of Nations in the East Indies*, Oxford: Oxford University Press.

Alteker, A. S. (2001) *State and Government in Ancient India*, New Delhi: Motilalal Banarsidass.

Armstrong, Karen (2002) *Islam: A Short History*, New York: Modern Library.

Aydin, Cemil (2018) 'What Is the Muslim World', *Aeon*, 1 August, https://aeon.co/amp/essays/the-idea-of-a-muslim-world-is-both-modern-and-misleading?__twitter_impression=true.

'Backgrounder: Five Principles of Peaceful Coexistence' (2015) *China Daily*, 22 April, www.chinadaily.com.cn/world/2015xivisitpse/2015-04/22/content_20509374.htm.

Baderin, Mashood A. (2000) 'The Evolution of Islamic Law of Nations and the Modern International Order: Universal Peace through Mutuality and Cooperation', *American Journal of Islamic Social Sciences*, 17: 2, 57–80.

Bain, William (2020) *Political Theology of International Order*, Oxford: Oxford University Press.

Bala, Arun (2006) *The Dialogue of Civilizations and the Birth of Modern Science*, New York: Palgrave Macmillan.

Bartelson, Jens (2018) *War in International Thought*, Cambridge: Cambridge University Press.

Basham, A. L. (2004) *The Wonder That Was India*, 3rd ed., London: Picador.

Bayly, Martin J. (2017) 'Imagining New Worlds: Forging "Non-Western" International Relations in Late Colonial India', *British Academy Review*, 30, 50–3.

Behera, Navnita C. (2007) 'Re-imagining IR in India', *International Relations of the Asia-Pacific*, 7:3, 341–68.

Belting, Hans (2011) *Florence and Baghdad: Renaissance Art and Arab Science*, trans. Deborah Lucas Schneider, Cambridge, MA: Harvard University Press.

Bennison, Amira K. (2009) 'The Ottoman Empire and Its Precedents from the Perspective of English School Theory', in Barry Buzan and Ana Gonzalez-Pelaez (eds), *International Society and the Middle East: English School Theory at the Regional Level*, Basingstoke: Palgrave, 45–69.

Bernal, Martin (1991) *Black Athena: The Afro-Asiatic Roots of Classical Civilization*, London: Vintage.

Boesche, Roger (2003) 'Kautilya's "Arthasastra" on War and Diplomacy in Ancient India', *Journal of Military History*, 67:1, 19–20, www.defencejournal.com/2003/mar/kautilya.htm.

Braudel, Fernand (1994 [1987]) *A History of Civilizations*, trans. Richard Mayne, London: Penguin Books.

Braudel, Fernand (2001) *The Mediterranean in the Ancient World*, trans. Sian Reynolds, London: Penguin Books.

Buckley, Chris (2014) 'Leader Taps into Chinese Classics in Seeking to Cement Power, *New York Times*, 11 October, www.nytimes.com/2014/10/12/world/leader-taps-into-chinese-classics-in-seeking-to-cement-power.html?auth=login-google.

Bull, Hedley (1966) 'International Theory: The Case for a Classical Approach', *World Politics*, 18:3, 361–77.

Bull, Hedley (1977) *The Anarchical Society: A Study of Order in World Politics*, London: Macmillan.

Bull, Hedley (1984) 'The Revolt against the West', in Hedley Bull and Adam Watson (eds), *The Expansion of International Society*, Oxford: Oxford University Press, 217–28.

Burbank, Jane, and Frederick Cooper (2010) *Empires in World History: Power and the Politics of Difference*, Princeton, NJ: Princeton University Press.

Buzan, Barry (2010) 'China in International Society: Is "Peaceful Rise" Possible?', *Chinese Journal of International Politics*, 3:1, 5–36.

Buzan, Barry (2011) 'A World Order without Superpowers: Decentred Globalism', *International Relations*, 25:1, 1–23.

Buzan, Barry (2014a) *An Introduction to the English School of International Relations*, Cambridge: Cambridge University Press.

Buzan, Barry (2014b) 'The "Standard of Civilisation" As an English School Concept', *Millennium*, 42:3, 576–94.

Buzan, Barry (forthcoming) *Global Society: An English School Structural History of Humankind since the Ice Age*.

Buzan, Barry, and Robert Falkner (forthcoming) 'The Market in Global International Society: A Dialectic of Contestation and Resilience', in Trine Flockhart and Zach Paikin (eds), *Rebooting Global International Society: Change, Contestation, and Resilience*, ch. 11.

Buzan, Barry, and Evelyn Goh (2020) *Rethinking Sino-Japanese Alienation: History Problems and Historical Opportunities*, London: Oxford University Press.

Buzan, Barry, and George Lawson (2014) 'Capitalism and the Emergent World Order', *International Affairs*, 90:1, 71–91.

Buzan, Barry, and George Lawson (2015) *The Global Transformation: History, Modernity and the Making of International Relations*, Cambridge: Cambridge University Press.

Buzan, Barry, and George Lawson (2016) 'The Impact of the "Global Transformation" on Uneven and Combined Development', in Alexander Anievas and Kamran Matin (eds), *Historical Sociology and World History: Uneven and Combined Development over the Longue Durée*, London: Rowman & Littlefield, 171–84.

Buzan, Barry, and George Lawson (2020) 'China through the Lens of Modernity', *Chinese Journal of International Politics* (online).

Buzan, Barry, and George Lawson (forthcoming) *Modes of Power: A Theory of International History*.

Buzan, Barry, and Richard Little (2000) *International Systems in World History*, Oxford: Oxford University Press.

Buzan, Barry, and Laust Schouenborg (2018) *Global International Society: A New Framework for Analysis*, Cambridge: Cambridge University Press.

Callahan, William A. (2009) 'Chinese Visions of World Order: Post-hegemonic or a New Hegemony?', *International Studies Review*, 10:4, 749–61.

Chaudhuri, K. N. (1985) *Trade and Civilisation in the Indian Ocean*, Cambridge: Cambridge University Press.

Chen, Yudan (2015) 'Chinese Notions of Sovereignty', in Jamie Gaskarth (ed.), *China, India and the Future of International Society*, London: Rowman and Littlefield, 38–52.

Chong, Ja Ian (2014) 'Popular Narratives vs. China's History: Implications for Understanding an Emergent China', *European Journal of International Relations*, 20:4, 939–64.

Christian, David (2004) *Maps of Time*, Berkeley: University of California Press.

Clark, Ian (2009) 'Towards an English School Theory of Hegemony', *European Journal of International Relations*, 15:2, 203–28.

Clark, Ian (2011) *Hegemony in International Society*, Oxford: Oxford University Press.

Cohen, Warren I. (2000) *East Asia at the Center*, New York: Columbia University Press.

Cottrell, Leonard (1957) *The Anvil of Civilization*, New York: Mentor Books.

Cox, Robert W. (1986) 'Social Forces, States and World Orders: Beyond International Relations Theory', in Robert O. Keohane (ed.), *Neorealism and Its Critics*, New York: Columbia University Press, 204–54.

Cui, Shunji, and Barry Buzan (2016) 'Great Power Management in International Society', *Chinese Journal of International Politics*, 9:2, 181–210.

Curtin, Philip D. (1984) *Cross-cultural Trade in World History*, Cambridge: Cambridge University Press.

Dalacoura, Katerina (2021) 'Global IR, Global Modernity and Civilization in Turkish Islamist Thought: A Critique of Culturalism in International Relations', *International Politics*, 58, 131–47.

Dalai Lama (2005) *The Universe in a Single Atom: The Convergence of Science and Spirituality*, New York: Morgan Road Books.

Dale, Stephen F. (2010) *The Muslim Empires of the Ottomans, Safavids and Mughals*, Cambridge: Cambridge University Press.

Darwin, John (2020) *Unlocking the World: Port Cities and Globalisation in the Age of Steam 1830–1930*, London: Penguin.

Datta-Ray, Deep K. (2015) *The Making of Indian Diplomacy: A Critique of Eurocentrism*, Oxford: Oxford University Press.

Deudney, Daniel (2007) *Bounding Power: Republican Security Theory from the Polis to the Global Village*, Princeton, NJ: Princeton University Press.

Dhammika, Ven. S. (1993) 'The Edicts of King Ashoka', Kandy: Buddhist Publication Society, www.cs.colostate.edu/~malaiya/ashoka.html.

Draper, Gerald (1995) 'The Contribution of the Emperor Asoka Maurya to the Development of the Humanitarian Ideal in Warfare', *International Review of the Red Cross*, 305, 30 April, www.icrc.org/en/doc/resources/documents/article/other/57jmf2.htm.

Dreyer, June Teufel (2016) *Middle Kingdom and Empire of the Rising Sun: Sino-Japanese Relations Past and Present*, New York: Oxford University Press.

Edwardes, Michael (1971) *East–West Passage: The Travel of Ideas, Arts, and Inventions between Asia and the Western World*, New York: Taplinger.

Eisenstadt, S. N. (2000) 'Multiple Modernities', *Dædalus*, 129:1, 1–29.

Fairbank, John King (1968) *The Chinese World Order: Traditional China's Foreign Relations*, Cambridge, MA: Harvard University Press.

Ferguson, Niall (2011) *Civilization: The West and the Rest*, New York: Penguin Books.

Garver, John W. (2016) *China's Quest: The History of the Foreign Relations of the People's Republic of China*, New York: Oxford University Press.

Gellner, Ernest (1981) *Muslim Society*, Cambridge: Cambridge University Press.

Gilpin, Robert (1981) *War and Change in World Politics*, Cambridge: Cambridge University Press.

Goh, Evelyn (2013) *The Struggle for Order: Hegemony, Hierarchy, and Transition in Post-Cold War East Asia*, Oxford: Oxford University Press.

Gray, Jack (2002) *Rebellions and Revolutions: China from the 1800s to 2000*, Oxford: Oxford University Press.

Gries, Peter Hays (2004) *China's New Nationalism: Pride, Politics, and Diplomacy*, Berkeley: University of California Press.

Hansen, Valerie (2012) *The Silk Road*, New York: Oxford University Press.

Harris, Stuart (2014) *China's Foreign Policy*, Cambridge: Polity.

Hitti, Philip K. (1962) *Islam and the West*, Princeton, NJ: D. Van Nostrand Company.

Ho, David Yau-fai (1976) 'On the Concept of Face', *American Journal of Sociology*, 81:4, 867–84.

Hobson, John M. (2004) *The Eastern Origins of Western Civilization*, Cambridge: Cambridge University Press.

Hodgson, Marshall G. S. (1993) *Rethinking World History: Essays on Europe, Islam and World History*, Cambridge: Cambridge University Press.

Holland, Tom (2012) *In the Shadow of the Sword: The Battle for Global Empire and the End of the Ancient World*, London: Little, Brown Book Group.

Hourani, Albert (1991) *Islam in European Thought*, Cambridge: Cambridge University Press.

Hu, H. C. (1944) 'The Chinese Concept of "Face"', *American Anthropologist*, 46:1, 45–64.

Hui, Victoria Tin-bor (2005) *War and State Formation in Ancient China and Early Modern Europe*, New York: Cambridge University Press.

Huntington, Samuel P. (1996) *The Clash of Civilizations*, New York: Simon and Schuster.

Hwang, Kwang-kuo (2011) *The Foundations of Chinese Psychology: Confucian Social Relations*, New York: Springer.

Jackson, Patrick Thaddeus (2010) *The Conduct of Inquiry in International Relations: Philosophy of Science and Its Implications for the Study of World Politics*, New York: Routledge.

Jackson, Patrick Thaddeus, and Daniel H. Nexon (2019) 'Reclaiming the Social: Relationalism in Anglophone International Studies', *Cambridge Review of International Affairs*, 32: 3, 582–600.

Jacq-Hergoualc'h, Michel (2002) *The Malay Peninsula: Crossroads of the Maritime Silk Road*, Leiden: Brill.

Kang, David (2003) 'Getting Asia Wrong: The Need for New Analytical Frameworks', *International Security*, 27:4, 57–85.

Kang, David (2003–4) 'Hierarchy, Balancing and Empirical Puzzles in Asian International Relations', *International Security*, 28:3, 165–80.

Kang, David (2005) 'Why China's Rise Will Be Peaceful: Hierarchy and Stability in the East Asian Region', *Perspectives on Politics*, 3: 3, 551-4.

Kang, David (2010) 'Civilization and State Formation in the Shadow of China', in Peter J. Katzenstein (ed.), *Civilizations in World Politics: Plural and Pluralist Perspectives*, London: Routledge, 91-113.

Kaplan, Morton A. (1966) 'The New Great Debate: Traditionalism vs. Science in International Relations', *World Politics*, 19:1, 1-20.

Katzenstein, Peter J. (2006) 'Multiple Modernities As Limits to Secular Europeanization?', in Timothy A. Byrnes and Peter J. Katzenstein (eds), *Religion in an Expanding Europe*, Cambridge: Cambridge University Press, 1-33.

Katzenstein, Peter J. (2010) 'A World of Plural and Pluralist Civilizations: Multiple Actors, Traditions and Practices', in Peter J. Katzenstein (ed.), *Civilizations in World Politics: Plural and Pluralist Perspectives*, London: Routledge, 1-40.

Kautilya (1915) *Arthashastra*, trans. R. Shamashastry, Bangalore: Government Press.

Kennedy, Hugh (2016) *The Caliphate*, London: Pelican.

Keohane, Robert O. (1988) 'International Institutions: Two Approaches', *International Studies Quarterly*, 32:4, 379-96.

Khadduri, Majid (1966) *The Islamic Law of Nations: Shaybānī's Siyar*, Baltimore, MD: Johns Hopkins Press.

Khaldun, Ibn (1969 [1370]) *Muqaddimah: An Introduction to History*, trans. Franz Rosenthal, Princeton, NJ: Princeton University Press/ Ballinger.

King, Amy (2014) 'Where Does Japan Fit in China's "New Type of Great Power Relations"?', *The ASAN Forum: Special Forum*, 2:2, 21 March, www.theasanforum.org/where-does-japan-fit-in-chinas-new-type-of-great-power-relations/?dat=March%20-%20April,%202014.

Kissinger, Henry (2011) *On China*, London: Allen Lane.

Kissinger, Henry (2014) *World Order*, New York: Penguin Press.

Kosambi, D. D. (1975) *An Introduction to the Study of Indian History*, Bombay: Popular Prakashan.

Koyama, Hitomi, and Barry Buzan (2019) 'Rethinking Japan in Mainstream International Relations', *International Relations of the Asia-Pacific*, 19:2, 185-212.

Krasner, Stephen (1999) *Sovereignty: Organized Hypocrisy*, Princeton, NJ: Princeton University Press.

Kulke, Hermann, and Dietmar Rothermund (1986) *A History of India*, New York: Dorset Press.

Lake, David A. (2009) *Hierarchy in International Relations*, Ithaca, NY: Cornell University Press.

Larson, Gerald J. (1998) *Classical Sāṃkhya: An Interpretation of Its History and Meaning*, New Delhi: Motilal Banarasidass.

Lawrence, Bruce B. (2010) 'Islam in Afro-Eurasia: A Bridge Civilization', in Peter J. Katzenstein (ed.), *Civilizations in World Politics: Plural and Pluralist Perspectives*, London: Routledge, 157–75.

Lawson, Fred H. (2006) *Constructing International Relations in the Arab World*, Stanford: Stanford University Press.

Lerner, Gerda (1986) *The Creation of Patriarchy*, New York: Oxford University Press.

Liebig, Michael, and Saurabh Mishra (2017) 'Introduction' in Michael Liebig and Saurabh Mishra (eds), *Arthasastra in a Transcultural Perspective: Comparing Kautilya with Sun-Zi, Nizam al-Mult, Barani and Machiavelli*, New Delhi: Institute for Defence Studies and Analysis, Pentagon Press, 1–30.

Little, Richard (2006) 'The Balance of Power and Great Power Management', in Richard Little and John Williams (eds), *The Anarchical Society in a Globalized World*, Basingstoke: Palgrave, 97–120.

Little, Richard (2007) *The Balance of Power in International Relations: Metaphors, Myths and Models*, Cambridge: Cambridge University Press.

Liu, Xinru (2010) *The Silk Road in World History*, New York: Oxford University Press.

Lustick, Ian S. (1997) 'The Absence of Middle Eastern Great Powers: Political "Backwardness" in Historical Perspective', *International Organization*, 5:4, 653–83.

Luttwak, Edward N. (2012) *The Rise of China vs. the Logic of Strategy*, Cambridge, MA: Belknap Press of Harvard University Press.

Lyons, Jonathan (2010) *The House of Wisdom: How the Arabs Transformed Western Civilization*, London: Bloomsbury.

Mackintosh-Smith, Tim (2002) *The Travels of Ibn Battutah*, London: Picador.

Mallavarapu, Siddharth (2009) 'Development of International Relations Theory in India: Traditions, Contemporary Perspectives and Trajectories', *International Studies*, 46:1–2, 165–83.

Mann, Michael (1986) *The Sources of Social Power*, vol. 1, Cambridge: Cambridge University Press.

McNeill, William H. (1965) *The Rise of the West: A History of Human Community*, New York: Mentor Books.

Menon, Sunil, and Siddhartha Mishra (2013) 'We Are All Harappans', *Outlook* (India), 13 August, 28–35.

Mitra, Sbrata K. (2017) 'Kautilya *Redux*?' in Michael Liebig and Saurabh Mishra (eds), *Arthasastra in a Transcultural Perspective: Comparing Kautilya with Sun-Zi, Nizam al-Mult, Barani and Machiavelli*, New Delhi: Institute for Defence Studies and Analysis, Pentagon Press, 31–62.

Moore, Gregory J. (2014) '"In Your Face": Domestic Politics, Nationalism and "Face" in the Sino-Japanese Islands Dispute', *Asian Perspective*, 38, 219–40.

Mulk, Nizam al (2002) *The Book of Government, or Rules for Kings*, Abingdon: Routledge.

Murphy, R. Taggart (2014) *Japan and the Shackles of the Past*, Oxford: Oxford University Press.

Nagao, Gajin M. (1991) *Mādhyamika, and Yogācāra, A Study of Mahāyāna Philosophies: Collected Papers*, trans. Leslie S. Kawamura, Albany, NY: State University of New York Press.

Narlikar, Amrita, and Aruna Narlikar (2014) *Bargaining with a Rising India: Lessons from the Mahabharata*, Oxford: Oxford University Press.

Nehru, Jawaharlal (1938) 'The Unity of India', *Foreign Affairs*, 16:2, 231–43.

Neumann, Iver B., and Einar Wigen (2018) *The Steppe Tradition in International Relations: Russians, Turks ad European State Building 4000 BCE–2017 CE*, Cambridge: Cambridge University Press.

Newbigin, Eleanor (2019) 'Do We Need to Decolonise History? And If So, How?', *History Extra* (BBC), 25 March, www.historyextra.com/period/modern/decolonise-history-curriculum-education-how-meghan-markle-black-study.

Odgaard, Liselotte (2012) *China and Coexistence: Beijing's National Security Strategy for the Twenty-First Century*, Baltimore, MD: Johns Hopkins University Press.

Ogilvie, Sheilagh (2011) *Institutions and European Trade: Merchant Guilds 1000–1800*, Cambridge: Cambridge University Press.

Onuma, Yasuaki (2000) 'When Was the Law of International Society Born? An Inquiry of the History of International Law from an Intercivilizational Perspective', *Journal of the History of International Law*, 2, 1–66.

Paine, Lincoln (2014) *The Sea and Civilization: A Maritime History of the World*, London: Atlantic Books.

Paine, S. C. M. (2003) *The Sino-Japanese War of 1894–1895*, New York: Cambridge University Press.

Phillips, Andrew, and J. C. Sharman (2015) *International Order in Diversity: War, Trade and Rule in the Indian Ocean*, Cambridge: Cambridge University Press.

Pelham, Nicholas (2016) 'The People Who Shaped Islamic Civilisation,' *The Economist 1843*, 5 December, www.1843magazine.com/culture/the-daily/the-people-who-shaped-islamic-civilisation.

Pines, Yuri (2012) *The Everlasting Empire: The Political Culture of Ancient China and Its Imperial Legacy*, Princeton, NJ: Princeton University Press.

Pines, Yuri (2018) 'Legalism in Chinese Philosophy', in Edward N. Zalta (ed.), *The Stanford Encyclopedia of Philosophy*, https://plato.stanford.edu/archives/win2018/entries/chinese-legalism.

Piscatori, James (1986) *Islam in a World of Nation-States*, Cambridge: Cambridge University Press.

Piscatori, James, and Amin Saikal (2019) *Islam beyond Borders: The Umma in World Politics*, Cambridge: Cambridge University Press.

Qin, Yaqing (2007) 'Why Is There No Chinese International Relations Theory?', *International Relations of the Asia-Pacific*, 7:3, 313–40.

Qin, Yaqing (2011) 'Relationality and Processual Construction: Bringing Chinese Ideas into International Relations Theory'; 'Rule, Rules, and Relations: Towards a Synthetic Approach to Governance', *Chinese Journal of International Politics*, 4:2, 117–45.

Qin, Yaqing (2016) 'Relational Theory of World Politics', *International Studies Review*, 18:1, 33–47.

Qin, Yaqing (2018) *A Relational Theory of World Politics*, Cambridge: Cambridge University Press.

Radhakrishnan, S. (1940) *Eastern Religions and Western Thought*, New Delhi: Oxford University Press.

Reid, Anthony (1988) 'Female Roles in Pre-colonial Southeast Asia', *Modern Asian Studies*, 22: 3, 629–45.

Ren, Xiao (2016) 'Idea Change Matters: China's Practices and the East Asian Peace', *Asian Perspectives*, 40, 329–56.

Ringmar, Erik (2019) *History of International Relations: A Non-European Perspective*, Cambridge, UK: Open Book Publishers, www.openbookpublishers.com/reader/228#page/150/mode/2up.

Risso, Patricia (1995) *Merchants and Faith: Muslim Commerce and Culture in the Indian Ocean*, New York: Routledge.

Rosenberg, Justin (2010) 'Problems in the Theory of Uneven and Combined Development Part II: Unevenness and Multiplicity.' *Cambridge Review of International Affairs*, 23:1, 165–89.

Rosenberg, Justin (2013) 'Kenneth Waltz and Leon Trotsky: Anarchy in the Mirror of Uneven and Combined Development', *International Politics*, 50:2, 183–230.

Rosenberg, Justin (2016) 'International Relations in the Prison of Political Science', *International Relations*, 30:2, 127–53.

Rudolph, Susanne Hoeber (2010) 'Four Variants of Indian Civilization', in Peter J. Katzenstein (ed.), *Civilizations in World Politics: Plural and Pluralist Perspectives*, London: Routledge, 137–56.

Ruggie, John (2004) 'American Exceptionalism and Global Governance: A Tale of Two Worlds?', Working Paper No. 5, Corporate Social Responsibility Initiative, Harvard University, April 2004.

Sarkar, Benoy Kumar (1919) 'Hindu Theory of International Relations', *American Political Science Review*, 13:3, 400–14.

Sarkar, Benoy Kumar (1921) 'The Hindu Theory of the State', *Political Science Quarterly*, 36:1, 79–90.

Sastri, K. A. Nilakanta (1967) *Nandas and Maurysa*, 2nd ed., New Delhi: Motilal Banarsidass.

Schneider, Louis (1970) *Sociological Approach to Religion*, New York: John Wiley.

Scott, James C. (2017) *Against the Grain: A Deep History of the Earliest States*, New Haven, CT: Yale University Press.

Shahi, Deepshikha (2014) '*Arthashastra* beyond Realpolitik: The "Eclectic" Face of Kautilya', *Economic & Political Weekly*, 49:41, 11 October, 68–74.

Shahi, Deepshikha (2018) *Kautilya and Non-Western IR Theory*, London: Palgrave Macmillan.

Shahi, Deepshikha (2020a) Book Review: *The History of the Arthaśāstra: Sovereignty and Sacred Law in Ancient India*, by Mark McClish, *Global Intellectual History*, DOI: 10.1080/23801883.2020.1771247.

Shahi, Deepshikha, ed. (2020b) *Sufism: A Theoretical Intervention in Global International Relations*, Lanham, MD: Rowman & Littlefield.

Shahi, Deepshikha, and Gennaro Ascione (2016) 'Rethinking the Absence of Post-Western International Relations Theory in India: "Advaitic Monism" As an Alternative Epistemological Resource', *European Journal of International Relations*, 22:2, 313–34.

Shambaugh, David (2013) *China Goes Global: The Partial Power*, Oxford: Oxford University Press. Kindle ed.

Sharan, Paramata (1992–3) *Ancient India Political Thought and Institutions*, Meerut, India: Meenakshi Prakashan.

Sharma, Ram Sharan (1996) *Aspects of Political Ideas and Institutions in Ancient India*, 4th ed., New Delhi: Motilal Banarsidass.

Sheikh, Faiz (2016) *Islam and International Relations: Exploring Community and the Limits of Universalism*, Lanham, MD: Rowman and Littlefield.

Shi, Yinhong (2007) 'The Need for a Composite Strategy in China-Japan Relations', in Gi-Wook Shin and Daniel C. Sneider (eds), *Cross Currents: Regionalism and Nationalism in Northeast Asia*, Stanford CA: Walter H. Shorenstein Asia-Pacific Research Centre Books, 213–25.

Shih, Chih-yu (1990) *The Spirit of Chinese Foreign Policy*, Basingstoke: Macmillan.

Shilliam, Robbie (2009) 'The Enigmatic Figure of the Non-Western Thinker in International Relations', *AntePodium: Online Journal of World Affairs*, https://nanopdf.com/download/robbie-shilliam-victoria-university-of-wellington_pdf.

Sil, Rudra, and Peter Katzenstein (2010) *Beyond Paradigms: Analytic Eclecticism in the Study of World Politics*, New York: Palgrave-Macmillan.

Simpson, Gerry (2004) *Great Powers and Outlaw States: Unequal Sovereigns in the International Legal Order*, Cambridge: Cambridge University Press.

Singh, G. P. (1993) *Political Thought in Ancient India*, New Delhi: D. K. Printworld.

Singhal, D. P. (1993) *India and World Civilization*, New Delhi: Rupa and Co.

Spruyt, Hendrick (2020) *The World Imagined: Collective Beliefs and Political Order in the Sinocentric, Islamic and Southeast Asian International Societies*, Cambridge: Cambridge University Press.

Suzuki, Shogo (2009) *Civilization and Empire: China and Japan's Encounter with European International Society*, London: Routledge.

Swope, Kenneth M. (2009) *A Dragon's Head and a Serpent's Tail: Ming China and the First Great East Asian War*, Norman: University of Oklahoma Press.

Tadjbakhsh, Shahrbanou (2010) 'International Relations Theory and the Islamic Worldview', in Amitav Acharya and Barry Buzan (eds), *Non-Western International Relations Theory: Perspectives on and beyond Asia*, London: Routledge, 174–96.

Tagore, Rabindranath (1918) *Nationalism*, London: Macmillan & Co.

Thapar, Romila (2002) *Early India: From the Origins to AD 1300*, New Delhi: Penguin.

Thapar, Romila (2012) *Ashoka and the Decline of the Mauryas*, 3rd ed., New Delhi: Oxford University Press.

Tickner, Arlene, and Ole Wæver (eds) (2009) *International Relations Scholarship around the World*. London: Routledge.

Tilly, Charles (1990) *Coercion, Capital and European States, AD 990–1992*, Oxford: Blackwell.

Towns, Ann (2009) 'The Status of Women As a Standard of "Civilization"', *European Journal of International Relations*, 15:4, 681–706.

Towns, Ann E. (2010) *Women and States: Norms and Hierarchies in International Society*, Cambridge: Cambridge University Press.

Tudor, Daniel (2012) *Korea: The Impossible Country*, Tokyo: Tuttle Publishing.

Turner, John (2009) 'Islam as a Theory of International Relations?' *E-International Relations Students*, 3 August, www.e-ir.info/2009/08/03/islam-as-a-theory-of-international-relations.

Wade, Geoff (2004) 'The Zheng He Voyages: A Reassessment', Working Paper Series No. 31, October, Asia Research Centre, National University of Singapore.

Walker, R. B. J. (1993) *Inside/Outside: International Relations As Political Theory*, Cambridge: Cambridge University Press.

Waltz, Kenneth N. (1979) *Theory of International Politics*. Reading, MA: Addison-Wesley.

Wang, Jisi (2011) 'China's Search for a Grand Strategy', *Foreign Affairs*, 90:2, 68–79.

Warner, Caroline M. (2001) 'The Rise of the State System in Africa', in Michael Cox, Tim Dunne, and Ken Booth (eds), *Empires, Systems and States: Great Transformations in International Politics*, Cambridge: Cambridge University Press, 65–89.

Watson, Adam (1992) *The Evolution of International Society*, London: Routledge.

Watson, Adam (1997) *The Limits of Independence: Relations between States in the Modern World*, London: Routledge.

Watson, Adam (2001) 'Foreword' to 'Forum on the English School', *Review of International Studies*, 27:3, 467–70.

Watson, Matthew (2018) *The Market*, Newcastle: Agenda Publishing.

Wendt, Alexander (1992) 'Anarchy Is What States Make of It: The Social Construction of Power Politics', *International Organization*, 46:2, 391–425.

Wight, Martin (1966) 'Why Is There No International Theory?', in Herbert Butterfield and Martin Wight (eds), *Diplomatic Investigations: Essays in the Theory of International Politics*, London: Allen and Unwin, 17–34.

Wight, Martin (1977) *Systems of States*, edited by Hedley Bull, Leicester: Leicester University Press.

Wight, Martin (1991) *International Theory: The Three Traditions*, edited by Brian Porter and Gabriele Wight, Leicester: Leicester University Press/Royal Institute of International Affairs.

Wilkinson, David (2008) 'Hêgemonía: Hegemony, Classical and Modern', *Journal of World-Systems Research*, 14:2, 119–41.

Yan, Xuetong (2011) *Ancient Chinese Thought, Modern Chinese Power*, Princeton, NJ: Princeton University Press.

Yan, Xuetong (2019) *Leadership and the Rise of Great Powers*, Princeton, NJ: Princeton University Press.

Yurdusev, Nuri (2004) *Ottoman Diplomacy: Conventional or Unconventional?*, Basingstoke: Palgrave Macmillan.

Yurdusev, Nuri (2009) 'The Middle East Encounter with the Expansion of European International Society', in Barry Buzan and Ana Gonzalez-Pelaez (eds), *International Society and the Middle East: English School Theory at the Regional Level*, Basingstoke: Palgrave, 70–91.

Zha, Jianying (2020) 'Prince Han Fei & Chairman Xi Jinping', http://chinaheritage.net/journal/chinas-heart-of-darkness-part-iii.

Zhang, Feng (2009) 'Rethinking the "Tribute System": Broadening the Conceptual Horizon of Historical East Asian Politics', *Chinese Journal of International Politics*, 2:4, 545–74.

Zhang, Feng (2014) 'International Societies in Pre-modern East Asia: A Preliminary Framework', in Barry Buzan and Yongjin Zhang (eds), *Contesting International Society in East Asia*, Cambridge: Cambridge University Press, 29–50.

Zhang, Feng (2015a) 'Confucian Foreign Policy Traditions in Chinese History', *Chinese Journal of International Politics*, 8:2, 197–218.

Zhang, Feng (2015b) *Chinese Hegemony: Grand Strategy and International Institutions in East Asian History*, Stanford: Stanford University Press.

Zhang, Yongjin (2001) 'System, Empire and State in Chinese International Relations', in Michael Cox, Tim Dunne, and

Ken Booth (eds), *Empires, Systems and States: Great Transformations in International Politics*, Cambridge: Cambridge University Press, 43–63.

Zhang, Yongjin, and Barry Buzan (2012) 'The Tributary System As International Society in Theory and Practice', *Chinese Journal of International Politics*, 5:1, 3–36.

Zhao, Suisheng (2017) 'Reconstruction of Chinese History for a Peaceful Rise', *YaleGlobal*, 13 June, http://yaleglobal.yale.edu/con tent/reconstruction-chinese-history-peaceful-rise.

Zhao, Tingyang (2006) 'Rethinking Empire from a Chinese Concept "All-under-heaven" Tian-xia', *Social Identities*, 12:1, 29–41.

Zhao, Tingyang (2009) 'A Political World Philosophy in Terms of All-Under-Heaven (Tian-Xia)', *Diogenes*, 221, 5–18.

Zhao, Tingyang (2014) 'The "China Dream" in Question', *Economic and Political Studies*, 2:1, 127–42.

Zhao, Tingyang (2015) 'Yi tianxia chongxin dingyi zhengzhi gainian: wenti, tiaojian he fangfa' ['Redefining the Concept of Politics via "Tianxia": The Problems, Conditions and Methodology', translated by Lu Guobin, edited by Sun Lan], *World Economics and Politics* (Beijing), 6, 4–22.

Zhao, Tingyang (2018) 'A Neglected Project for Tianxia System', paper presented to the international conference on Global IR and Non-Western IR Theory, China Foreign Affairs University, 24 April.

INDEX

Printed in the USA
CPSIA information can be obtained
at www.ICGtesting.com
LVHW011828221223
767237LV00007B/371